Jakub's World

Jakub's World

A Boy's Story of
Loss and Survival in the Holocaust

Alicia Nitecki

and

Jack Terry

Afterword by Jörg Skriebeleit

STATE UNIVERSITY OF NEW YORK PRESS

Published by
State University of New York Press, Albany

For information, address State University of New York Press, 90 State Street, Suite 700, Albany, NY 12207

Production by Diane Ganeles
Marketing by Fran Keneston

Library of Congress Cataloging-in-Publication Data

Nitecki, Alicia, 1942–
    Jakub's world / by Alicia Nitecki and Jack Terry.
        p. cm.
    ISBN 0-7914-6407-5 (hardcover : alk. paper) — ISBN 0-7914-6408-3 (pbk : alk. paper)
    1. Szabmacher, Jakub. 2. Jews—Poland—Kazimierz (Pulawy)—Biography. 3. Jewish children in the Holocaust—Biography. 4. Holocaust, Jewish (1939–1945)—Poland—Kazimierz (Pulawy)—Biography. 5. Kazimierz (Pulawy, Poland)—Biography. I. Terry, Jack, 1930–. II. Title.

DS135.P63S93855 2004
940.53'18'092—dc22   2004016209

10 9 8 7 6 5 4 3 2 1

Dedicated
to the memory of Major Feliks S. Kurnatowski, #12274 Flossenbürg
and to
Colonel Louis S. Leland and Ruth M. Leland

Cruelty has a Human Heart
And Jealousy a Human Face
Terror, the Human Form Divine
And Secrecy, the Human Dress

The Human Dress is forged Iron
The Human Form, a fiery Forge
The Human Face, a Furnace seal'd
The Human Heart, a hungry Gorge.

—*William Blake*

Contents

Acknowledgments

The title essay, "Jakub's World," appeared in the *Massachusetts Review 38* (4) (Winter, 1997–98).

We owe a special debt of gratitude to Maj. Samuel S. Gray, Jr. (d. March 22, 2003), and his family for giving us access to his privately published *Letters to Martha*, his letters from Flossenbürg to his wife, and to Douglas Salter for offering us his uncle Capt. Dr. W. Lawrence Salter's papers and taped recollections.

Jakub's World

Five-year-old Jakub Szabmacher sits on the floor in the center of the front row of a group of children posing for a photograph. He wears a Little Lord Fauntleroy velvet suit and lace collar and he looks very sulky.

Jakub's sulkiness is not unusual. He's known to his family as a "little devil," a "rascal," a "scamp." He always wants his own way and when he doesn't get it, he throws tantrums—never in front of his father, even though his mother's long thin hands are the ones that really hurt when he's slapped.

He's given to willful excess. He stands in the pouring rain outside his aunt's house for half an hour because his mother has refused to buy him what he wants. His mother ignores him but his big sister, Dewora, gets soaked trying to coax him back inside. His pride won't let him give in to her too quickly, but he's gratified to see how much she cares.

When his mother takes him with her to visit Mala Kirszt, the midwife who brought him into the world and who is now dying of cancer, he keeps up an even whine: "I want to go home. I want to go home. I want to go home," and then when his mother, Bluma, doesn't respond, he pokes his finger into an electric light socket—electricity is a luxury in his town—and gets stuck to the lamp. He nearly electrocutes himself.

When he's old enough to know better, he whines and sulks because his mother tells him that she cannot afford to buy him the tin of shoe polish he wants. She knows he's picky about his appearance. Hasn't she marvelled that in spring when the unpaved streets of his village turn to ankle-deep mud his boots stay clean? He beats up bigger boys. Their mothers come to his house to complain. They glance at the skinny little fellow and say his stocky older brother Hiluś has been out there slugging their sons. He'll probably grow up to be a bandit, his family sighs. He hates his home town Bełżyce. Hates the unpaved streets, the boring, gossipy people. When he's big enough, he's going to leave. Go to his father's hometown Warsaw, perhaps, like his brother Hiluś and his sister Dewora. His earliest memory is of his father taking him there when he was three and he still remembers the names of the streets: Chłodna, Nowolipki. His father brings chocolate tortes filled with mocha cream and pale plywood boxes filled with golden smoked sardines back with him from Warsaw—you can't buy food like that in Bełżyce!

Or to Kazimierz, his mother's family home where her sister, his aunt, has a bakery and where he spends his vacations. Kazimierz has paved streets, a cobbled market square, beautiful baroque houses—on one of them there's a bas relief of St. Christopher with the Christ child on his shoulder—and the best ice cream in the world. People from all over Poland vacation in Kazimierz, visit the wooden synagogue to see the Esterka's crown, which King Kazimierz Wielki gave to his beautiful Jewish mistress, Esterka. Kazimierz Dolny, on the Vistula River, is "*czyste jak pudełko*," clean as a box, he hears people say. In Kazimierz, he swims in the broad and winding Vistula river, climbs steep grassy slopes to the white castle which looks down on the town. He takes walks with his mother along a road that leads up a hill and they drink in the scent of acacias each spring and he piles up glossy horse chestnuts there in the fall. Yes, Kazimierz, perhaps.

Or . . . "Jakub has told us, 'When I am eighteen years old, I'm going to Palestine,'" his father, Chaim, writes to his sister who is living there.

In the meantime, he has to live in Bełżyce, small, drab Bełżyce—even the bus he takes to Kazimierz doesn't bother to exhibit its name—where there's a mill and a forge, a few small shops and businesses catering to the surrounding farms and the town, and a bar where men drink, and where Jakub knows everyone, at least by sight. Mr. Goldstein has a long beard, wears a hat. He trains the little orthodox boys of Bełżyce in the Torah, the alphabet. Jakub goes to the Tarbut school, he doesn't attend the Cheder, but he looks up to Mr. Goldstein. Mr. Goldstein's a teacher, and Jakub knows that a teacher must have his respect. The old lady in black he often sees in the square lifts her skirts, spreads her legs, and pisses in the street. One of the neighbors has a peg leg and hangs a piece of burlap out on the line to dry every day. It is common knowledge to Jakub and his friends that this grown-up wets his bed! Mrs. Chómicka is his mother's friend. Nojech Feld, the watchmaker, is a communist. Srulke Kirszt, the barber who pulls teeth as well as shaves chins, stands outside on his verandah when he's drunk and bellows out arias. Blacksmith Skrajinski's grown-up son, Mietek, is bulky and strong. He got that way, Jakub's mother has told him, from eating up all his scrambled eggs, and his mother should know, they rented rooms in the Skrajinski's house when Hiluś was a baby and they had more money. Most of Bełżyce, Jakub finds, is primitive, small minded, un-nice.

He lives at 9 Ulica Krótka, Short Street, at the edge of the center of town. The neighborhood is mixed: Jews and non-Jews live harmoniously together. The family occupies one large room of a small wooden house with carved corner posts, an open front porch with a little peak-roofed attic above it, and an outhouse at the back. There is a well across the street by the forge and they wash in the cold water from that well even in winter. It helps to keep him healthy, his mother says. A large bed stands against one wall in their room and opposite it an armoire, a pot bellied stove, and a wooden linen chest. When relatives come to stay, they set a board and a mattress on four chairs for them to sleep on.

A lilac tree grows right outside their front window and when they open it lilacs pour in. In spring, he stands by the window carefully picking through the sprays for three- and five-petalled flowers, then sucks the drop of sap at their base. Jakub likes that tree, its taste and its smell, and he likes the sour cherry tree that stands to the right of the house and whose branches he climbs to pick the delicious tart fruit; the raspberries, currants, and gooseberries that grow at the side; the wild blueberries he picks in the woods; and the fresh yellow tomatoes farmers give him when he goes to nearby villages, hamlets, and farms with his father's relatives the Kirszts, who fit glass into windows.

When he's very young, he sits on his great-grandfather's lap and sucks sugar cubes that the 102-year-old man dunks in vodka for him. When he's bigger, he chases hoops; plays *Pietnaście Kroków* (I reached you in fifteen paces—you're out!); collects big black beetles after it has rained from the ground by a shed in the market square, traps them in match-boxes, holds them to his ear and listens to them scratch; gouges birch twigs into whistles; makes skates in the winter by taking a triangular piece of wood, heating up a wire and burning it into the edges of the wood, then nailing straps onto the wide part. Most of the time they don't work too well but it keeps him busy and it's fun. He plays cards with Uszer Weisbrot, Moiszele Friedman, and Herszel Zancberg, the fuel merchant's son. They are older than he is, but he always wins.

Jakub is afraid of the dead. When someone in his neighborhood has died, he imagines the corpse will reach out and grab him, so he runs past that house as fast as he can, holding his breath.

He can't wait to grow up and do the things his older brother does—go to school, wear long trousers, play chess with his father. His father is a middle man supplying goods to local shops, he goes away frequently to Warsaw and when he comes back Jakub meets him at the bus stop and kisses his hand. None of the other children greet their fathers like that! None of his friends call *their* parents *Tatunia, Mamunia,* or address them politely using the formal third person.

Jakub notices that Chaim reads *Der Hajnt,* a Zionist daily, that Bluma subscribes to a Polish language Jewish weekly, *Opinja*, that *Opinja* comes from Warsaw. Jakub is too little to know that the same cooperative publishes both, that they are both Zionist publications loyal to the Polish government, openly patriotic even, that *Opinja* is written in Polish because its editors wish "to raise a curtain and reveal to the Polish community, with whom we share the same piece of earth, a mirror in which it can see a faithful image of the Jewish community," and that "its chief aim is to acquaint the Jewish inteligentsia which reads Polish with the broad field of Jewish knowledge, with the deeds of the Jewish nation, with the pearls of Hebrew and Yiddish literary creation."

He's proud of his father. "My father can run fast, faster even than the fireman on his way to a fire! That's how fast he ran chasing those gentile kids across the meadow when they threw stones at us last Saturday!" Jakub brags to his friends. Firemen often run through Bełżyce. The houses there are always catching on fire. The last great fire took out half the town and some of the old people when asked when they were born say, "in the year of the last great fire."

"My father is a good mother!" he says the time his mother goes to Warsaw for a week, to see a doctor about headaches which blind her with rings of light, and someone wonders aloud in front of him what kind of time the family's having now that their mother is gone.

His father is highly thought of: people respect him, trust his judgement, consult him, ask his advice. He knows his father is an expert at packing. When a family moves to Palestine they come to ask for his help.

After Hiluś has left home and is living in Warsaw, his father sits and reads the Bible to Jakub on Friday nights, teaches him to read. Jakub reads the story of Joseph and cries over the part where his brothers put the young boy in the well.

He wants to excel at reading, like Hiluś. He's heard his mother boast that Hiluś was reading *Pan Tadeusz* by Mickiewicz and knew parts of it by heart! He's jealous. He fears his mother loves his brother the best.

He's deeply attached to his mother. He looks like Bluma, people say, the same brows, blue eyes, high cheekbones, the same shy smile. He has trouble falling asleep unless she lies down by his side. He rests his arm across her chest and is comforted by her warmth, by the texture of her skin. Once, walking down the street with his sister Miriam, he looks back and sees her standing on the porch in her blue dress patterned with forget-me-nots watching them go. He recognizes her look, it's her loving look. He averts his face and walks on, secure in her love.

He likes to spend time with her, watch her go about her work, hear her hum strains of Dvořák and Schubert (he doesn't know those names), sit on the linen chest by the stove as she cooks. The chest is taller than he is, he scrambles on to it carelessly one day and wounds his wrist on a knife. The scar never does go away.

His mother is powerful. She, too, commands respect. Once when he and his mother were out taking their usual walk down that hill in Kazimierz, a gentile boy threw a stone at him and missed, and, then, Jakub threw a stone back and bloodied the kid's face. Grown-ups came at them with pitchforks, yelling "Lousy Jews!" until one of the men recognised his mother, remembered her from school, and the pitchforks came down, the group dispersed.

Jakub has a vague sense that his family is poor partly because some of the shopkeepers don't pay his father what they owe for the wares he supplies and his father is unwilling to press them hard for their debts. But what can young Jakub know of the economic distress in the village, of the backbiting and gossip, of the neighbor who worries out loud to Chaim that soon he may be out of work; of the man who emigrates to Palestine taking three thousand *zloty* from the till at the bank, and whose wife maligns Chaim by telling someone that he will be to blame if Palestine sends him back? What does the child know of his own parents' lives, of his father's failed attempts to move them all to Palestine, of the everyday worries and concerns which Chaim spells out in letters to his sister Bracha in Palestine, such as the one he sent her in 1936?

Forgive me for not writing sooner. . . . I forwarded your letter to Warsaw. Now, I am back there fetching Miriam because she was there on vacation and now must go back to theTarbut. . . . I have no news. Nothing is any better. . . .
I already went to Betar [to try to get a visa to Palestine], but couldn't find Zaiczyk, and it's a waste of time to talk to anyone else. It's all over. As hard as it is, we must forget it. . . .
As for the family in Bełżyce, there's no news. Things are as they were. I had to send the children to the Tarbut and must pay tuition. I don't know where I'll get it, but what can you do?
My Hiluś is going into the sixth grade. He's a good student, and Jakub speaks only of you. *He'll* go to Palestine.
Itzak wrote me that he works hard and earns £16 a month. He can be sure that in Poland, he wouldn't even earn £1 a month.
Tell Yechiel Persik that I and Yosele are happy that he's already in Palestine because he suffered enough.
Things are no better with Mala [who has cancer]. It should only happen to Hitler!

Jakub knows only that when the family is together, there is nowhere he would rather be. He likes the family dinnertimes when his mother puts out bowls of sweet, waxy potatoes and sour milk, or a bowl of barley and mushroom soup, and his parents and he and Hiluś and Dewora and Miriam sit down together at the table and eat and talk and giggle over each other's warm and silly banter. Should Jakub's name be spelled Jakub or Jakób? Should Dewora be referred to as Szabmache*równa*? No! Not Szabmacher*ówna*, that rhymes with "gówna" (shit)! "Hello, Herszel, is it still snowing outside?" Chaim always asks when the neighbors' boy comes into the house on warm summer days.

Jakub likes rainy summer nights when he and Miriam carry straw mattresses up the steep narrow staircase to the attic above the porch and he lies listening to the rain falling on the tin roof of the house and knowing that his parents are down there in their room. When Jakub is with his family like this, he is complete in a completeness he has no need to explain.

On the September 1, 1939, Jakub sees planes fly above his village. Lublin is bombed. Hundreds of people are dead. On September 16, German trucks, armored cars, and tanks appear in Bełżyce, men wearing fitted leather caps and goggles sit inside. German soldiers walk into Bełżyce shops, take whatever strikes their eye, especially from the Jews, leave notes in German to fill the gap: *Die Wahre ist mein, der Zettel ist dein, wenn der Krieg zu Ende ist, dann wird alles gut sein.* (The goods are mine, the receipt is thine, when the war has ended, then everything will be fine.) German voices bar Jewish children from attending school after third grade, order Jews to wear a white band with a blue star of David on their arms, impose rationing, levy money from the Jews, send the Jewish men of Bełżyce to clear, to mend roads. Posters appear on the stands and walls of Bełżyce on which red letters form Polish words to mouth the German equation *Żydzi-Wszy-Tyfus Plamisty* (Jews-Lice-Typhus).

Jakub hears the men talk about the German invasion of Poland, reminisce about the First World War, feels the uncertainty in the air, but for the boy the planes, the tanks, the soldiers in the square are action, novelty, excitement.

It is calm in Bełżyce in the fall of 1939. Every day Jewish merchants open those small gray and brown shops which edge the town's vast, muddy square. Every day Jewish tradesmen go on plying their trades. Every day the old woman in black still walks down the street; the barber shaves chins, sings in the bar; the peg-legged young man still hangs out his sheet; Herszel Zancberg can still be seen chopping wood for his father; Bluma Szabmacher still chats with Pani Skrajinska, Pani Chómicka, discusses Goethe with Chaim's cousin, Szya Weller, the saddler. Every day the town seems the same.

But something has altered. New details have emerged. German soldiers are encamped in the town square. Groups of Jewish men with shovels and pickaxes are out working on the roads, singing a song as they work:

> *Marszałek Śmigły-Rydz*
> *Nie dał nam nic, a nic.*
> *Ale Hitler drogi*
> *Dał nam roboty.*

> (Marshal Śmigly-Rydz
> Gave us nothing, nothing at all,
> But dear Hitler
> Gave us hard labor.)

Small Jewish boys stand around the square during the day. Chaim Szabmacher no longer travels to Warsaw. He sits at home, he sits with his friends, he reads the papers, he discusses the news.

Jakub hangs around the soldiers, he polishes their boots, he sometimes brings home a loaf of heavy, dark, German army bread. Quite something that loaf of bread! He's in seventh heaven when he brings it home. He hangs around the barber's shop, sweeps the floor, brushes hair from customers' shoulders, lathers chins with suds; he learns to shave. He brings the groszy home. Once, when Miller Woźniak's son, back home on a visit from America, stops by the Barber's, he tips Jakub a whole *zloty!* Jakub's the youngest, he's only nine, but his father's out of work and Hiluś is in Warsaw, so he's the family's breadwinner now. He's filled with pride.

One day, Jakub notices that Mr. Goldstein has shaved his beard, that Mr. Goldstein has removed his hat; hears that Mr. Goldstein, the Cheder teacher, is working with the Germans. This is the boy's first great disillusionment.

The winter of 1939–40 is the coldest in the living memory of Bełżyce. The Jews are now responsible for providing crews to clear snow from the roads. Jakub hires himself out as a stand-in, the family needs the groszy he earns. Hiluś and Dewora return home bringing with them stories of the bombardment of Warsaw. Rumors start reaching town that the Jews from some of the neighboring towns are being driven out, that ghettos are being formed, that the Germans are beating the Jews, that such things are happening in Lublin, in Pulawy; that Jews in Kazimierz are being rounded up, that there is such panic among them that they are afraid to take in refugees.

Jakub doesn't hear these rumors, but one night Bluma ties a kerchief around her head like the peasant women do and sets out in the darkness to walk thirty-five kilometers across the fields to Kazimierz, carrying a bag of flour to give to her sister there.

Meanwhile, Bełżyce stays calm, dreadfully calm.

And then on a bitterly cold and snowy Friday evening in mid-February, one of the coldest in the living memory of Bełżyce, horse-drawn sleds drag 600 Stettin Jews from Lublin to Bełżyce. The short distance has taken them all day and the hands and feet of many people, children among them, are frost-bitten. The sleds stop at the synagogue where the Jews of Bełżyce have been instructed to receive them.

Jakub walks across the frozen town with Chaim to help unload the sleds. The child is bewildered and appalled by what he sees. A mass of people, Jews like him, with children like him among them, stiff from a day's journey on an overcrowded sled, so numb with cold that they can barely move by themselves, some so frost-bitten that they are lying on the ground unable to rise are moaning, crying. Chaim and other men help them off the sleds, carry them into the synagogue, help take those unfortunate people to shelter in other people's houses. Then, saddened and depressed, return home.

They did not expect this, despite the boxed notice in *Opinja* on August 6, 1939, which alerted readers to the situation of those Jews who, having been thrown out of Germany in October, 1938, had come to Lwów:

> Citizen. How can you sit yourself down at the table with your family, when you know that your brother from Germany, who maybe yesterday was richer than you, is literally dying of hunger? With what kind of conscience do you plan outings, frequent places of entertainment, send your family, or yourself, to beach resorts, and don't consider for a moment that those most unfortunate of the unfortunate, victims of terror and bestiality, have no roof over their heads? . . . The poor and unhappy Jewish deportees from Germany, who are literally starving, call on their brothers to persuade them to share with them a piece of dry bread.

Despite the questions the same issue of the paper raised about the fate awaiting the children of Poland's German-Jewish refugees: "Why are these likable, nice, talented children suffering? What will become of them, what can become of them? What still awaits them?"

Despite the Germans bivouacked on Bełżyce's muddy square.

Despite the German plunder of Jewish shops.

Despite the doors of schools being barred to Jewish children.

Despite their nine-year-old youngest child, the boy who had so much wanted to learn, spending his days brushing hair off German shoulders and dust off German boots. Despite all of this, the plight of Europe's Jews, and the war, had, until now, seemed almost abstractions to the Szabmachers. Today, they had all seen it. Seen the unwanted Jews of Stettin with yellow Stars of David on their breasts—those *verfluchte Juden*, *Żydzi-Wszy-Tyfus Plamisty*, those polluters of the Reich—old people, young people, rich people, poor people, children, babies in arms, pulled along the frozen rutted roads hungry, numb, frost-bitten, half-dead, and unloaded, like refuse, in the center of Bełżyce.

The sight of these people sends Chaim reeling into the darkest reaches of the self, blinds him to the woman and the children seated with him at the table. Jakub sees tears in his father's eyes and hears his forty-four-year-old father say, "I will now consider that I have reached my three score and ten and that my life is at an end." These desolate words on this desolate day marking Chaim's withdrawal into private pain and fear mark for the boy the moment of his father's fading to the periphery of family life.

Bełżyce lies about twenty kilometers southwest of Lublin, some forty kilometers east of the Vistula river, and some hundred kilometers west of the River Bug, on a high limestone plateau where fields of wheat, soy, rye, and hops alternate with dense forests, peat bogs, and meadows that, at certain times of the year, hold water.

The village arose at the point of intersection of a web of roads, one of which in the Middle Ages took people from Kraków to Wilno. Its location on this road made it a halting stage for merchants travelling to the Lublin Fair as well as a rallying point—for the clans of gentry who held musters there in the fifteenth century; for the Polish Brethren who had a school and a meeting house there during the Reformation. The first of the Jews who settled there arrived at the beginning of the sixteenth century, and one of them, a certain Jakób, became famous for his disputations with the antitrinitarians.

For a brief period over the centuries of its existence, Bełżyce acquired the status of town, but by the beginning of the twentieth century it was again no more than a settlement, a large village, whose council had jurisdiction over people who lived in the nearby area.

For centuries the population of Bełżyce farmed, labored, kept small shops, traded, sold their wares and their work to the neighboring country people who, in turn, brought their produce to the rectangular marketplace that formed the village's hub—a marketplace so large that it dwarfed the already low, single- and two-story undistinguished shops and houses, some stuccoed, some wooden, on its periphery. The size of the population, which had held fairly steadily at the three-thousand-some mark for more than a hundred years, suddenly increased to 5,664 in the decade between 1921 and 1931. This sharp increase brought with it a housing shortage: whole families occupied single rooms. Half of Bełżyce's residents at that time were Jewish.

The marketplace, the few houses built along the spokes of the many roads crossing the town, a church, a spring, two synagogues, a forge, and a mill were all there was to the village.

On the flat, unprepossessing, isolated land dotted with insignificant villages, hamlets and lone cottages where Bełżyce may be found—land the Germans claimed as theirs, land which ends at the Ribbentrop-Molotov line—the Germans decided to contain the Jews of the Reich.

"This area with its very swampy character could, in the estimation of District Governor Schmidt, serve as a reservation for Jews," the Nuremberg Trials show Seyss Inquart saying at a conference in Lublin on November 20, 1939. "Such a measure," he added, "could possibly bring about a decimation of the Jews."

They created a private park, as it were, a preserve on which and from which they could draw at will, a preserve fenced in, at first, with words instead of wire.

And it was as a result of this decision, that the Jews from German Stettin had been brought to Bełżyce and made the responsibility of the two-thousand-some Jews of that town.

The housing situation in Bełżyce, already difficult before the war, had been rendered worse by the continuous arrival of individuals and families seeking refuge in still peaceful Bełżyce from the maltreatment and the ghettos the Germans were already creating in other towns and villages in the Lublin area. Although some of the refugees still had the wherewithal to support themselves, or had families living in Bełżyce who could, and were willing, to support them, others needed help from the larger community and, in Bełżyce, that community, although not yet destitute, was poor. The correspondence, preserved in the archives of the Jewish Historical Institute in Warsaw, between Bełżyce and the main offices of the Jewish Social Self-Help Organisation in Kraków reveals the situation in which the Jewish population of the town, the refugees, and the newly arrived transport of Jews from Stettin, found themselves. The Polish Jews wrote on February 6, 1941:

> Already in 1939 our poor small town took in many refugees whose number increased at the beginning of 1940 together with the six hundred evacuees from German Stettin. At the same time the number of poor residents increased, bringing the number of poor to a terrible five hundred as compared to the two thousand people who make up our poor town. We have reached the point that for every two residents there is one evacuee or poor person. Ignoring this, however, we tried to organize help with our own resources: we set up a community kitchen, a collection of clothing, footwear, a sanitary patrol to deal with various illnesses.
>
> Our greatest difficulty was with the matter of accommodations because of the great shortage of housing which has existed here since before the war.

The letter continues:

> We overcame even this difficulty. When the Joint [Distribution Committee] became acquainted with the extent of our action they apportioned a monthly subsidy for us which we received until May 1940. After that, the subsidy from the Joint

was reduced to a minimum. As a result the level
of our action was significantly lowered and the
refugees and the poor are condemned to hunger
in cold clay dug-outs whose walls are dripping
moisture, this has had an effect on the state of
health of our little town where sickness and death
have become our frequent guests.

After the Stettin Jews arrive, Jakub still works at the
barber's shop, still substitutes on the roads, still brings
the few *groszy* he earns home to his mother. The family is
still together and, even though they have had no regular
income for quite some time, his family manages somehow.

In May, for the first time, the Germans come to Bełżyce
demanding men: the *Judenrat* must supply them with three
hundred Jews. Hiluś Szabmacher is one of those picked.

Jakub does not see his brother loaded onto a truck and
taken to one of the four workcamps opened in spring 1940
in the village of Józefów forty kilometers southwest of
Bełżyce on the Vistula River, but he comes home to find
Hiluś gone and his mother so distraught that he thinks
she's gone mad. She rushes around their room collecting
together anything which has the remotest value—the green
patterned plush cloth on the family's table, the green patterned plush cover from their bed. She rushes out to sell
them. She needs the money to use as a bribe with which to
persuade the Germans to restore her first-born child to her.
The money is not enough; Bluma fails.

Jakub has never seen his tall, slender mother as desperate as this; he's always seen her independence, strength,
and her pride. He's only just turned ten, and he's not old
enough to understand exactly to what kind of place Hiluś
has been taken; not old enough to understand that his
brother could be killed. He's only old enough to be self-
centered, to consider what this event will mean for him,

and, at this moment, he feels more excluded from his mother's concern than he has ever felt. A saddened Jakub takes her frenzy and fear for Hiluś as irrefutable evidence that she loves his brother more than she loves him. The demands on the already burdened Jews of Bełżyce continue to increase. Now they must obey a curfew, they must not go out on the streets in the evening; they must not eat white bread; they must not eat meat. At the end of 1940 they are commanded to close their shops and relinquish their wares. Possession of meat, possession of wares are punished with death.

Regularly now gray-uniformed gendarmes come from nearby Niedrzwica, the nearest railway town, to impose German laws on Bełżyce, to take monetary contributions, horses, wagons; to kill.

Regularly now Gestapo man Kurt Engels, district prefect, arrives from Lublin. He is a man of medium height and build, dressed in a civilian suit with a Nazi pin in his lapel, and a pistol in his pocket. He drives into Bełżyce, he steals, he robs. He, too, demands contributions. He, too, kills.

Engels walks into the barber's shop where Jakub is working.

"*Wie heißt du?*"

"Jakub Szabmacher."

"*Wo hast du den deutschen Namen gestohlen?*" (Where did you steal the German name?) he barks at the very frightened boy, then orders him to clean his car.

Jakub knows that Engels is a killer, that a scratch on Engels's car might cost him his life. He goes cold when the newly shaved Engels inspects the job and accuses him of cleaning only one side of the car:

"*Rasiert dein Kusine nur eine Seite?*" (Does your cousin only shave one side?)

Engels is given to such quips. Jakub hears him say to Eugen Heymann, an older boy from Stettin who is a member of the Jewish Police, "*Du bist ein guter Jude, ich werde dich als letzten erschießen.*" (You are a good Jew, I will shoot you last.)

Engels walks freely into Jewish houses, peers into pots, checks for meat and white bread, and, if he finds them, shoots. He kills the round-faced boy of fourteen or so who is wearing a white open-necked shirt, a gray jacket, and a peaked cap tilted a little to the left at the back of the photograph in which Jakub is sulking. He kills not only that straight-backed boy, Jankiel Silbernadel, but also his brother, Uszer, and his father, Kune Hersz, because the meat being carried in a bag down a road in Bełżyce is traced as having been bought from them.

By the beginning of February 1941, "the number of poor is higher than the number of the averagely placed and we are helpless in this situation," the local *Judenrat* tells Kraków.

The refugees want a little warm food and a piece of bread but all this is an impossible fantasy. The accommodation situation has worsened because a large number of places have lost the ability to take anyone in, and if the future brings us continuing waves of refugees then fifteen people will have to be housed in rooms 4 x 4 meters in size.

The working of the Joint is limited and in light of that we are turning to the Jewish Social Self-Help in Kraków with an urgent plea. Save a large number of refugees and poor from hunger as fast as possible. Allot us an appropriate subsidy taking into account the deserving nature of our little town which supports the downtrodden with its last groszy and is coming to the limit of its strength. We live in hope of a fast and positive response to our appeal.

Please note: the deportees from Stettin are writing separately. . . .

In their letter of the same day, the Stettin deportees wrote:

Every day we cater to about 210 people by serving
black coffee and dry bread in the mornings and
evenings and a warm soup for lunch which con-
tains almost nothing but water. Since we are no
longer able to raise money ourselves, we implore
the Jewish Social Self Help which basically took
over the function of the Joint to support us with
money and food. If we do not get help soon, the
consequences will be terrible. Most of the people
who have died lately, have died of hunger or the
extreme cold in unheated quarters.

Chaim, Bluma, Dewora, Miriam, and Jakub are joined
in their room on Krótka Street by Chuna Zweig, an older
brother-in-law of Chaim's, who has fled Warsaw where he
worked on the Jewish newspaper, *Der Hajnt.* He stays with
them for a few months, amazing Jakub with his ability to
hold a glass of boiling hot tea to his lips. The Szabmachers,
like the rest of Bełżyce, feel the strictures of life under
German occupation ever more keenly. They rub the bread
that now constitutes the main part of their diet with garlic.
They have nothing else to put on it, and even if they were
allowed the butter Jakub loves, the butter that they used to
buy wrapped in moist cabbage leaves, and even if they
could afford it, they would have nowhere to buy it. The
Germans have ordered crews of Jews to dig the mud, to
seed grass and plant trees on the ground where the market
used to be held.

The sense of novelty and pride Jakub once felt about
contributing to the family purse, has turned into a sense of
desperate necessity. The *groszy* are not enough. He goes to
work as a cowherd on a peasant farm in the vicinity of Bełżyce.
He will be out of the way of the Germans and he will be fed,
the family agrees, and there will be one mouth less to feed
at home.

So, just after the wheat and the rye have been reaped,
Jakub leaves his home in Bełżyce to live by himself on a

small peasant farm, one of several such isolated farms, set amid miles of small, unhedged, fields distinguished from each other by the texture and the color of the crop they bear: drab yellow stubble where the grain has been cut, dark green where potatoes and beans still grow. Now one squat tree dots the flatness, now a thin line of them underscores it. Occasionally, a stretch of forest fills the horizon.

He rises at daybreak with the half dozen cows he tends and takes them into a field to pasture. Often, in the heat of those late summer days, a cow, feeling exuberant, arches its tufted tail into the air and takes off into other men's fields at high speed, followed by the rest of the herd. Jakub has to give chase then, run across the stiff stubble which cuts his bare feet like a razor. The chase is painful. It makes the boy cry, but if he doesn't divert the cows back to their rightful pasturing place, the peasants he works for beat him.

The routine of his lonely days is broken by the presence of small, barefooted, local gentile boys who, like him, are minding other men's herds. He bands together with them, they talk, sometimes they roast potatoes over fires of dried cow dung in the fields.

He stays outside with the cows until evening when he returns them to the barn, eats his evening meal outside by himself, then goes back into the barn to sleep. Jakub is still just a young child and when he has trouble, as is normal for him, sinking into sleep, he does not find comfort in the animals breathing and stirring around him. He misses his mother.

Periodically, as payment for his labor, Jakub is given a bag of potatoes or beans, which he carries back to his family.

The visits home intensify Jakub's loneliness. Even though his father sits depressed, his mother anxious about Hiluš and worn with care, their room is clean and inviting, their exchanges are loving and civilized. The peasants he works for are crude, coarse, and indifferent. They fart, they belch, they hit. The food they eat—great pots of cabbage or beans cooked with cubes of pork fat—though plentiful and welcome, is different from the food he eats at home. The farm he returns to is dirty; the floor of the barn in which he sleeps is a wet, boggy, mass of cow dung and urine-drenched straw. The land on which it is set, bearing the stamp of centuries of arduous human labor, does not entice Jakub's imagination to run carefree and wild, nor his heart to recognize companionship with it, for all the presence of the other small boys.

After a few weeks there, he breaks under the weight of his sickness for home. No matter that at home food is scarce, no matter that at home he is prey for the Germans, he would prefer, he realizes, to go to his death with his family than live here safely alone. He runs away. Away from the farm, across the fields, back to Chaim, back to his elfin-faced sister and playmate Miriam, back to his beloved, beautiful, motherly Dewora, back to Bluma's love and warmth. His family welcomes him home.

In August 1941 the Germans establish a concentration camp outside of Lublin in Majdanek; in November, they establish a concentration camp at Belzec. That fall, they set up a workcamp in the forests in Poniatów, a village twenty-one kilometers west of Bełżyce, where thousands of people are put to work sewing garments and repairing roads. As a result, in Bełżyce, at this time, the first large round-ups begin. *Uwaga! Uwaga! Achtung! Achtung!* the loudspeakers summon the Jews to assemble and to file past an SS commander who selects from their midst the ones that he wants. Several hundred are deported to Poniatów. Chaim's brother-in-law, Zweig, and barber, Kirszt, for whom Jakub works are sent in the first large group to Majdanek.

On May 11, 1942, Chaim Szabmacher is taken in another mass deportation. Jakub sees open trucks crammed with men drive north out of town. When he gets home his father is gone.

Refugees from various parts of Poland continue arriving in the village; the Germans continue to bring in large transports of Jews. Twelve hundred people are transported from Leipzig to Bełżyce. The poverty and hunger continue to get worse, and again the German Jews write to Kraków: "We are running the kitchen for 600 persons and are forced to raise this to 1,500 to meet minimal need . . . we need double the amount of medicine because there are a lot of sick people among the new refugees. Is it possible for you to send straw mattresses because people are having to sleep on the bare ground even in the hospital?"

The poverty in the Szabmacher house has increased to the degree that Bluma appeals to the Jewish social organization for a coat, and when Jakub asks her what he should put on his bread, she responds simply: "Your teeth."

Chaim's sister, Sara Spiewak, and her little son, Imek, who is about four years old, have fled their home in Warsaw and are living with them now. Little Imek is lively, alert, he runs around asking "*Co to jest? Co to jest?*" ("What is that? What is that?") to the amusement of his cousins who, when the questioning gets too much for them, chant back, "*Co to jest? Czy to koń, czy to pies?*" ("What is that? Is it a horse, is it a dog?")

They open the door one evening to find that Hiluś has come back from Józefów labor camp west of Bełżyce where he had been used to mend dikes by the Vistula river. He is filthy, he stinks. They do not allow him inside until they have helped him wash at the well and he has put on clean clothing. Then they feed him whatever they have, listen to him talk about the camp, about being punished, about being made to sit upright for hours, through the night, sometimes, on the wet ground. But the Germans have not killed Hiluś. The Szabmacher children are together again. Perhaps Chaim, too, will return.

The large transports of deported Jews continue to arrive, and now, too, Polish Jews from the surrounding countryside are ordered to move to Bełżyce. Rumors start to circulate that the Germans are going to deport all the Jews and people start to find hiding places for themselves against such an eventuality. Some dig tunnels beneath their houses; some make trap doors; some block in cellars; one man digs a space beneath the horse in his stable for a Jewish girl to hide in. Bluma sends Miriam and Jakub to the safety of a gentile acquaintance's loft where they stay for a couple of days before the loneliness for their mother and their home hits them both with the same intensity it had hit Jakub on the peasant farm and, safe or not, they decide to go back and, if need be, die with their mother.

Sobibór opens, the third concentration camp in the province of Lublin. More work camps appear on the spoke of roads leading out of Bełżyce: Nałęczow, Radawiec Duży, Niedrzwica; small camps are added to those in Józefów, Poniatów, and, thirty-eight kilometers further south, one in Budzyń near Kraśnik. Ghettos are being cleared in Chodel and Opole. The rumor grows more persistent that Bełżyce is to be emptied of Jews. The Szabmacher family decides again on places to hide: Bluma, Dewora, and Miriam will join communist Nojech Feld in the hideaway he has not left since the Germans first came in; Hiluś will hide in a culvert by the small river that flows near their street; Jakub, his Aunt Sara and her little son Imek will go to shelter with their relatives, the glaziers.

> The situation in Bełżyce is desperate. "The need is getting bigger and bigger," the Social Self-Help group informs Kraków on August 13, 1942. "The *Judenrat* which is the only institution able to provide help, currently caters for 900 people in the emergency kitchen, serving morning coffee and lunch and is no longer able to fulfill its duties. Over the past 14 days it not only had to provide for the poor people of the town and the emergency kitchen but also had to support the kitchen for the work camp."

Three weeks later, on September 2, 1942, they write again: "Sadly enough, you did not answer and we did not get any support. The situation, on the other hand, has gotten worse, if that is possible. The situation is so bad by now that each day several people starve to death. Our own means and efforts are depleted, we have to give up unless you help us soon. "Help us quickly and help us fundamentally."

On September 14, 1942, the Kraków office responds:

> We acknowledge receipt of your letter of the second of the current month and inform you that unfortunately because of a lack of funds we are unable to come to your aid at the present time. We are aware of the hard situation in which you find yourselves, in spite of that, and with the best will in the world, we cannot come to your financial assistance. We are hopeful that in a very short time we will have at our disposal a small amount of food stuffs as a result of an exchange for sardines received from overseas Jewish charitable organisations and we will try, when we share them out, to take your town into account.

On September 23, Kraków replies for the last time:

> We are hopeful that in the near future we will have at our disposal, as a result of an exchange for sardines, a small amount of Maggi soup extract.

The correspondence ceases.

Before dawn on October 12, 1942, the people of Bełżyce are awakened by gunfire outside their village. The first rumor says that it is the gentile Poles who are going to be taken away; the second rumor says, no, the Jews. Jews go into hiding. SS men and Ukrainian soldiers in their employ enter the village.

When they walk into her room early that October morning, Bluma Szabmacher, with remarkable self-possession, asks the Ukrainians (in the Russian she speaks well) if they would like a glass of vodka. She wants to give her family time to disperse. Jakub, Imek, and Sara Spiewak run to glazier Kirszt's house. Jakub hears the glass shards in their loft crunch and crackle beneath his feet as his relatives tell them to go away, that there is no room for them there.

With nowhere else to hide, the three of them are forced to join the press of Jews being marched to the railway station in Niedrzwica. The column is long; the road is crowded; the people are desperate. "Have you seen my mother?" Jakub asks, running up and down the marching line searching for Bluma and his sisters, and, when he doesn't find them, tells his aunt he is going to try to run away. As the column passes a bend in the road by a stretch of dense forest, he runs up an embankment and between the trees. The Ukrainians shoot; he manages to escape, lies low for some time. The following morning, he puts his ear to the ground, listens, and, hearing no one coming, runs back into Bełżyce.

The village is silent. The loudspeakers have stopped announcing "*Uwaga! Uwaga! Achtung! Achtung!* The penalty for hiding Jews is death. The penalty for looting is prison." The house searching has ended. The Jews who were discovered have been taken away. The SS and the black-uniformed Ukrainian soldiers have left. Those they chose to kill lie on the ground. In an empty lot on the eastern side of the market square, at the other end of the village from the culvert in which he was supposed to be hiding, Jakub finds Hiluś lying dead. A single bullet has penetrated his right cheek. Mietek Skrajinski had pointed him out to a Ukrainian as he crouched in the culvert, and the Ukrainian routed him out with the end of his rifle, a gentile Pole tells Jakub. Brave eighteen-year-old Hiluś grabbed the rifle away and ran. Ran in the direction of the village where his mother and sisters were hiding. Ran into a Ukrainian trap. Was shot.

Bluma, Dewora, Miriam, the Felds, and the people who owned the house in which they were all hiding could hear the commotion, the shooting, the screaming in the street below.

All of them heard the shot that killed Hiluś.

"That bullet," Bluma said, "sounds as though it went into a human being."

A man peering out through a crack in the wall of the hideaway saw who it was who had just been shot, but could not bring himself to tell Bluma that it was her own son who had fallen.

Jakub makes a decision. His mother must not be told that Hiluś is dead. He, Dewora, and Miriam pick their brother up, push him in a wheel-barrow to the Jewish cemetery and bury him there themselves.

Witnesses report that when it reached Niedrzwica, the column of Jews from which Jakub had escaped was put into freight cars whose floors were covered with quicklime. The doors were closed and sealed. The train was sprayed with chlorine.

Sara and Imek Spiewak were not brought as far as Majdanek.

The Jews who have survived the killings and the mass deportation are ordered to move into the synagogue and its adjoining houses which have been surrounded by a barbed wire fence. Bełżyce is now a workcamp. Mr. Goldstein is made its leader, he is responsible for collecting the rent the Germans are charging: two thousand *zloty* from each family. The Jewish *Ordnungspolizei* are ordered to see to it that the Jews stay there. Meanwhile, as usual, the Jews are to work mending roads.

As usual, the gendarmerie, the Gestapo, and the SS visit the camp and, among them now, fat, tall, attractive, SS-*Obersturmführer* (Lieutenant) Amon Göth appears, imposing in his glittering officer's uniform. He collects the Jews together in the main hall of the synagogue, rests his right foot on a chair and in his slow, deliberate, and very clear voice tells them:

"*Alle Schmuck muss abgegeben werden.*" (All jewelery must be surrendered.) Bluma begins to slip from her finger her broad wedding band worn thin by years of wear.

"Give it to me," Jakub tells her, "I will hold it and, if they notice, I will drop it onto the floor."

He saves the wedding band, but he is not able to save Miriam when, in November 1942, Göth comes back to Bełżyce, murders seventy-six people and claims her for Poniatów along with eight hundred others.

Even though he knows some of the men and boys who lie down near him at night in the area designated for men in the hall of the synagogue in workcamp Bełżyce—Herszel Zancberg is with him there—Jakub's sense of foreboding sends him into the women's quarters. He is twelve now, but he still needs Dewora and Bluma's warmth.

That winter, two Jewish men who had been taken from Warsaw to Sobibór escape from there and find their way to Bełżyce. From them, the population of the camp learns about gas chambers.

That winter and spring, the Germans continue building and enlarging their camps, among them, the *Zwangsarbeitlager* in Budzyń, a subcamp of Majdanek, which is to be moved across the street to an open field and, in place of the original eight, forty barracks are projected to contain the prisoners needed by Heinkel Aircraft Company to manufacture bombers. To command the camp, they bring in from Camp II, the extermination compound, in Belzec, one of its three commanders—SS-*Unterscharführer* (Sergeant) Reinhold Feix, a not-quite-thirty-year-old former barber from Neudorf in the Sudetenland. A graduate of the SS training camp at Trawniki, he wears an automatic pistol on a string around his neck, and has a cherubic face.

That spring, it is rumored that the then-mayor of Bełżyce, one Stanisław Szubartowski, has said that for his upcoming Nameday he would like to be rid of the Jews.

Perhaps it is only a coincidence but in the season of Pentecost, at dawn on May 8, 1943, the day after St. Stanisław's day, Sergeant Reinhold Feix leaves his private apartment at Budzyń, assembles twenty-four of the Ukrainian soldiers who work for him, and heads north with them for Bełżyce.

"*Alle Juden raus!*"

The Jews are routed from the synagogue and the houses. Some of the Ukrainian soldiers are positioned around the periphery of the camp. The question flashes through Jakub's mind, "Why don't some of the men, or the bigger boys, grab one of their machine guns?" No one does. No one can.

The selection begins.

Feix separates the men from the women. He chooses several men among them to dig graves. He divides the young boys from the men. Orders the men to stand to one side of an outhouse in rows of five. He orders the boys to lie face down, one next to the other, in a line on the ground on the other side. He opens a flask of vodka, takes a few swigs.

As he is lying there, Jakub watches Feix walk along the row of boys, shooting each one through the back of the head. One of the little boys lying near him shouts out to his father, *"Tate! Tate! Nem mein broit"* ("Daddy! Daddy! Take my bread.") Noticing that the ground beneath the outhouse has eroded, leaving a gap, Jakub waits until Feix has turned his face away from his end of the line, then bellies his way underneath the outhouse and out to the lines of men on the other side. The men standing in one of the rows let him sneak in. The boy places stones beneath his feet to make himself look taller.

Most of the men are ordered back inside the synagogue.

Outside the synagogue, a few Jewish men are ordered to dig two massive graves. Feix selects out the younger women. Ukrainians chop the heads off infants and the toddlers they snatch from the mothers. The older ones are lead in small groups to the back of the synagogue. Those awaiting their turn hear shots. When Feix and the Ukrainians have finished 700 Jewish women and 150 Jewish children are dead.

As the men and the remaining young women are marched out of Bełżyce, someone tells Jakub that his sister had refused to be parted from her mother, and that as a reward for her loyalty, Feix shot her first in full view of Bluma, and then he murdered their mother.

Jakub's world has collapsed and expired.

Abraham Szabmacher, Jakub's great-grandfather.

Bluma Szabmacher, back row right.

Chaim Szabmacher.

Deworah Szabmacher, on right.

Miriam Szabmacher.

Purim, Bełźyce, Herszel Zancberg
(in fireman's helmet) second from left second row.
Deworah fourth row center.

Tarbut school, Jakub fifth from left, front row.

Darkness

Now standing in wooden wagons pulled by horses, now walking holding the wheels of empty wagons to steady them on hills, the remaining Jews of Bełżyce move south down familiar dirt roads through a familiar countryside past villages with familiar names: Kępa, Skoczyce, Urzędów. The familiar road is strange now and offers no comfort. It leads to an end they neither know nor look for. That intense moment by the synagogue that obliterated their past makes their future unthinkable and suspends them in the present, a terror.

The blood of their dead comes to Budzyń first: on a Mercedes diesel SS car, on SS uniforms, on SS Sergeant Feix's hands—"dirty blood," "Jews' blood." Washed off with water, it soaks into the camp's earth.

Then the living come. A few families—Manfred Heymann with his brother and both parents, luckier than others, perhaps because they were German, not Polish, Jews, as he himself suggested in the testimony he gave in 1955 (preserved in the Jewish Historical Institute in Warsaw). Vestiges of families, mainly: Pola Grinbaum-Kronisz and her sister, parents, and three brothers murdered in Bełżyce by Feix; Herszel Zancberg and his father, mother, and sister murdered in Bełżyce by Feix; Jakub by himself, his brother dead in Bełżyce; his father absorbed into the depths of Majdanek; his sister Miriam held in Poniatów; his mother and sister Deworah murdered in Bełżyce by Feix.

35

Jakub sees a guardhouse in front of a gate at the end of a tree-lined path, sees an open square, four guard towers, a row of windowless barracks, sees black-uniformed Ukrainian guards; sees Feix. As the people walk into the camp, Feix decides fifty more of them are unfit to work. Herszel Zancberg sees the jacket his father had been wearing wheeled back on a wagon into the camp.

The original settlement of forty-three brick houses, residential hotel, bathhouse, co-op to which the German occupiers of Poland had given the name Bydzyń had been constructed in 1937 as part of the Polish government's effort to industrialize the nation in an economically deprived, sparsely populated area of forests, fields, and meadows to house workers at a new ammunitions factory. At the beginning of September 1939, when Germany invaded Poland, the Poles cleared the factory and evacuated the workers. In the summer of 1941, when Germany invaded the Soviet Union, the Germans constructed a row of wooden stables for their horses in a clearing at one edge of the little settlement. By mid-1942, an affiliate of the Heinkel Aircraft Company had taken over the empty ammunitions factory and the SS administrators of Lublin took over the stables to house the Jews who they were going to send to work there.

From among the four thousand Jews they were deporting from nearby Kraśnik at the time of the Feast of the Tabernacles (late September 1942), they selected a thousand stronger ones for Heinkel, taking the rest to Sobibór and Belzec to kill them. "We built the camp—put up the barracks and horse stalls, and a barbed wire fence," Izchak Lamhut testified after the war. To the original row of stables they added a kitchen, a bath, a barracks for women separated by its own wire fence, a latrine at the corner of the compound next to one of the four guard towers; a guard house at the entrance in front of the gate leading into the camp. A wooded area divided the *Zwangsarbeitslager* (hard-labor camp) from the little settlement in which lived the

German Croatian civilians employed at the Heinkel plant. At the edge of the woods they built barracks for the SS, and in a couple of the brick houses facing the path into the camp they established the *Lagerführer's* office and residence. From the Lipowa Street prison in Lublin, they transported around fifty Jewish-Polish prisoners of war, among them tall, red-haired Noah Stockmann whom they made camp elder. He was a thoroughly decent man; interceded with Feix on his fellows' behalf; attempted to keep people's spirits up. Samuel Zylberstajn in his memoir remembers Stockmann saying to him and other new arrivals from the Warsaw Ghetto as he paints red crosses on their jackets and pants at Feix's order: "Don't upset yourselves. We'll outlive him."

From the camp in Janiszów after the Partisans had killed the camp's leader in October 1942, the Germans went and fetched the remaining prisoners to Budzyń. At the beginning of 1943, they brought people in from Hrubieszów. In April and May 1943, "After the burning of the [Warsaw] ghetto the remaining survivors were taken to Treblinka. A part of them, to which I belonged," David Spiro, a member of the Rabbinical Council of the Israelite Cultural Council told the Bavarian CID in 1968, "were diverted to Lublin." In Lublin, an unnamed witness testified, "We were told to sit on the ground near the train. There were Jews here from countless places all over Poland." And then, Spiro said, "appeared one day SS-staff Sgt. . . . Feix . . . who selected 800 men from our transport for the Budzyń ZAL."

In a snapshot printed in the 1995 issue of *Regionalista*, journal of the Kraśnik Regional Society, Reinhold Feix stands holding a cigarette in one hand and his other hand in his pocket laughing with a bespectacled SS-man who has both hands in his pockets. The day is sunny, both are in uniform but not in their greatcoats. Feix's six-year-old son stands in front of his father wearing long socks, short trousers and a miniature SS jacket. He is blond and round faced like his father, and he too holds one hand in his pocket, the other hand at his side. Feix sometimes likes the boy to watch

when he shoots Jews; on this occasion the three males standing there are sharing a joke. It's not clear what it is they are
looking and laughing at.

There is a sense of well being, a slight swagger in Feix's
casual posture, a touch of the theatrical—Noël Coward
perhaps—in the way he holds the hand with the cigarette
just above the shiny belt buckle at his waist, a touch of
blatancy about his round, laughing face. But his character
cannot now be read from his image, just as his character
could not then be read from his face, "He had a good-
natured, angel's face," one of his captives recalled. "He in
no way had the face of a criminal," another one said. His
hand is remembered holding a flask of vodka; his hands are
remembered held at his belly as he struts between the rows
of new arrivals to the camp; his hands are remembered
holding an automatic pistol, a cat o'nine-tails, a horsewhip,
a club.

His was the presence that defined and haunted Budzyń
hard labor camp for Jews, and the statements made after
the war in Poland, Germany, Holland, England, the United
States, and Israel, by men and women who had been held
in Budzyń form an accusatory litany, a continuous repeti-
tion of the name of Feix:

"Of the guard detachment I remember especially well
Feix...."

"At this time in Budzyń camp an SS-man by the name
of Feix was the camp commandant.... Other members of
the camp personnel I cannot remember."

"Other than Feix—I can no longer remember the
names of the Germans...."

"The camp commandant at that time was the notorious SS-Q-master Sergeant Feix. He was replaced ... by an
SS-2d Lieut. whose name I no longer remember."

"I remember very well everything about Feix during
his visit to the fuel-dump camp."

"I know that Feix killed people daily...."

"Feix shot a camp inmate, name unknown, on the first
day of his duty in Budzyń."

"He made it his daily habit to come into the camp hospital and there to look for people to exterminate."

"Feix was a sadist who would whip, shoot, or torture for his own amusement."

"I myself have seen how Feix actually flayed a prisoner alive with his riding-whip. "

"In the ZAL Feix had himself shot many prisoners."

"I myself was a witness when Feix shot Jews."

"I have frequently seen how Feix set his big Alsation dog on a prisoner with the shout: 'Seize him!' "

"I was personally beaten about the face with a riding-whip by [Feix] during my stay in this camp practically every morning at roll-call . . . and injured in so many ways the blood flowed. In addition he stamped on my toes with his jackboots."

"I know that Feix killed people daily. . . . He beat people, shot them, hanged and burned them."

"During my time as a male nurse, Feix came every second or third day into the barracks to see who was incapable of work. . . . Feix made sure that the sick who were incapable of work for too long a time were killed."

"I can't get rid of the horrifying image of the German, Feix—the camp Kommandant—setting that Jewish manufacturer on fire. . . ."

"The SS-man Feix . . . was constantly present in my husband's thoughts until the day he died."

The men and women crammed into the seven wooden barracks that form Budzyń *Zwangsarbeitlager* take stock not just of Sergeant Feix's larger gestures, his outer physical form, but even of the subtler aspects of his nature: that he prefers the German to the Polish Jews; that he has some grudging respect for a uniform; that he has a phenomenal memory for faces; that he is not so strong. That the barber from the Sudetenland may not feel entirely secure in his position.

The people in these barracks give him various soubriquets: he is known as *"Schweinhund,"* as *"Sauhund,"* as "Dr." Feix because his remedy for sickness is death. He is a murderer, a criminal, a butcher, and when the language of ordinary human life proves too poor to encode him they resort to images from fiction, mythology, and fable: he is a "sadist" who "demands human sacrifices day after day," "who had to kill at least two people before breakfast every day because otherwise he would have lost his appetite," a vampire who "always demanded fresh blood."

On the morning after he has brought the Jews of Bełżyce to Budzyń, Feix pulls Jakub and other boys out of the lines, but Stockman manages to persuade the *Kommandant* that although they are small, the boys can be useful, can work, and Jakub, like Herszel is sent across the road to build barracks.

Many of the prisoners, women as well as men, work at the Heinkel factory constructing airplane parts, or in its warehouse carrying iron pipes; some work as electricians laying cables and wires from the settlement to the factory; some build barracks for the new camp; some are used by a private firm installing central heating at the factory; some build roads; garden in the settlement and at Feix's residence where young Chaim Arbajtman from Warsaw is employed planting cabbages in beds shaped like a swastika. The more fortunate work in the hospital, or, better yet, the kitchen. All of the prisoners as they parade out to work must sing—sentimental Polish songs: *"Wszystko mi jedno"*— (It's all the same to me); spirited ones: *"Idzie dziewcze po lesie, po lesie, po lesie"* (A girl is walking through the forest, through the forest, through the forest); tangos, such as "Marianna," and, sometimes, it pleases one SS man to hear "My Yiddishe Mama" sung by Jewish boys whose mothers he and his fellows have murdered.

The camp is small, overcrowded, intimate. The men and women held there frequently know one another. Many of the people from the ghetto in Warsaw know each other, know that a man Feix orders the Ukrainians to beat when they stand at Appell is a Professor Herzl; know details about each other's lives; know that an elderly man Feix shoots to death is Dr. Pupko; know, as Zylbersztajn does, that Dr. Pupko had been a good man, "who after he had made a visit to a poor sick person always left money for him to buy medicines and food." Jakub, Herszel, and all the other men and boys from Bełżyce sleep five to a bunk in Barracks 5. Jakub meets a Rabbi Stockhammer there who, when he learns the boy's last name is Szabmacher, tells him he had met his father Chaim in Warsaw.

Some people are there with remnants of their families—brothers, sisters, fathers, mothers.

The people from Bełżyce know the forests in this area well, and this intimacy makes some attempt to escape. Some succeed. Feix rushes around like a Fury, then shoots into barracks, rounds up his Ukrainians, and for each escapee, drags ten people from Bełżyce out of the barracks. Sometimes he beats and bloodies them, picks some among the beaten and shoots them. Sometimes he makes them lie face down on the ground all night, anyone who moves is beaten and kicked; some are killed, some survive, have to be hospitalized; some are shot by Feix.

Jakub and all the people in Budzyń are caught, as it were, on a spotlit stage beyond which all lies in blackness; characters trapped in a drama of death directed by Feix, a drama in which he makes them participate.

One inmate, Isak Ehrenberg, sees Feix order another prisoner "to ram a garden hose into the mouth of another prisoner and to pump him so full of water that he eventually burst."

The entire camp stands helpless in the small Appellplatz. In the center five men are kneeling. Feix walks behind them, shoots each one in the back of the head. One after another of the men drop to the ground.

They stand in formation in the Appellplatz on May 25, 1943 when Feix finds out that a man from Warsaw named Bitter had a few *zlotys* and a watch belonging to his wife hidden in the false bottom of his eating dish. Feix orders one of his Ukrainian sergeants to tie a cord around Bitter's neck and to drag him by that cord in front of the assembled prisoners, and makes them participate in murder. He orders the prisoners to hit Bitter, but not hard. The penalty for not hitting, and for hitting too hard, is death. Bitter falls down under the thousands of light blows, is dragged along the ground, dragged to the steps of a barracks, drenched with water, revived, dragged around, and hit again. Although some of them want to put the man out of his misery, no prisoner dares to hit Bitter hard enough to kill him: they are not allowed to and no one chooses to die.

And on that spotlit stage, little escapes the eyes of Feix. "He recognized among us in Budzyń," Róza Mittelman said, "women he'd ordered to stay in Bełżyce . . . he shot them with his own hands." When he's riding on his horse one day, he notices as he passes Herszel Zancberg that the youth is wearing shoes without socks, demands to know what has happened to the socks he remembers him wearing the last time he saw him. "My shoes are too small, my feet have swollen," Herszel tells him. "Did you sell the socks?" Feix raises his hand, slashes the youth across the face with his crop. Herszel's ears ring for weeks after that.

Jakub cleans houses for the *Luftwaffe* and *Wehrmacht* in the settlement at the end of the path; carries out buckets of urine and excrement from a house occupied by a German *Feldtwebel* and his Polish girlfriend; cleans cars for a German airman who knocks him half senseless against a wall when he accidentally pushes a button once and the car jumps.

He watches hungrily as his one relation there, his uncle, husband of his mother's sister in Kazimierz, eats a loaf of bread without giving him a crumb. He sees sisters and mothers in the women's barracks, some of whom work in Germans' houses, passing food through the wire to their sons, brothers, and husbands, and wishes he had a mother or a sister there.

He derives some comfort from the presence in the barracks of Herszel, Rabbi Stockhammer, and his friend Rabbi Shapiro, and of a tall, imposing man from Warsaw, his father's age, called Luksemburg who has part of one finger missing and who takes him under his wing at work.

Acutely aware of his reduction to *Untermensch*, Jakub even feels pleasure when, as he parades out to work past *Oberscharführer* Willi Kleist one day, the SS man refers to him by name and teases him with a dirty question, *"Jakob, hast du schon einmal gevögelt?"* (Have you ever fucked?)

But the feeling that dominates and stifles all others is fear, for everywhere Jakub looks he sees beatings, killings, and death.

As Zylbersztajn writes "Throughout the whole stay in the camp there was never a moment at which one of us could say, 'Now, I'm at peace, I am not threatened by death.' Nothing helped, neither adhering strictly to orders, nor maintaining discipline. It was simply a matter of luck."

Sometimes, people are transported to Budzyń from other camps in the Lublin area, bringing news with them. Sometimes brothers are re-united, friends meet friends from their home town or village. Once someone newly arrived in Budzyń gives Jakub a note from Poniatów: "I know what has happened." his sister Miriam has written, "My only wish is to see you again."

And just as a flash of lightning momentarily reveals details of a landscape hidden by a leaden, cloud-heavy sky, so Miriam's note pierces through the curtain Budzyń has drawn across his mind, and Jakub sees his mother, father, Deworah, Hiluś, Miriam, all of them as they had been, longs for them, feels their loss. Then Budzyń intervenes and blocks them from his view.

Spring turns to summer, some of his Ukrainian guards go into Feix's lodgings when he's not there, take valuables and money looted from the Jews on behalf of the Reich, take weapons and ammunition, flee. Feix turns to Lublin for help. The search goes on day and night. Feix turns to vengeance, orders twenty-nine prisoners, Herszel Zancberg among them, to lie face down on the ground, the guards to trample on them, but Noah Stockman intervenes: "Wait until Sunday to make an example of them," he suggests, "everyone will be here inside the camp then." Feix concedes. The search goes on. The thieves cannot be found. On Sunday, the prisoners are told to assemble, but witness, not the punishment of their fellows, but prisoner Aleks Einhorn on the guitar accompanying prisoner Shmulek Goldstein from Warsaw singing a farewell to Feix. Rumor has it that their *Lagerführer* (the sergeant) is being sent to the bane of the SS, the Eastern Front.

Nothing changes for the prisoners in Budzyń as a string of *Lagerführer*'s come and go in Feix's place: Werner Mohr, of the *Schutzpolizei* (Security Police); SS-*Oberscharfürher* Fritz Tauscher, lawyer; a man called Franz; SS-*Obersturmführer* Josef Leipold, barber from Saxony. Their deputies: *Unterscharführer* Ernest Teufel; *Oberscharführer* Willi Kleist; Adolf Axman; Adolf Gross. One *Kommandant* is short, the other tall; one young, the next old; but the shootings, beatings, and killings continue—they all bear the same stamp as Feix's.

And in this later period of his incarceration in the camp, Jakub has impressed on him again a lesson in how human beings behave when threatened. Somebody from one of the barracks escapes. The SS line the prisoners up in columns of five and walk through the rows counting: one, two, three, four, and, when they get to five, shoot. One, two, three, four, five—shoot. Nobody wants to be in front. The crowd of people, like cattle, like some kind of animal, stampedes to get out of the way. Nobody wants somebody else to be killed, but no one wants to be killed.

Summer turns to fall, and at the beginning of November, some Polish workmen in the factory, some people bringing supplies to the camp from Lublin, pass terrible news on to some of the people in Budzyń: The SS have held an *Erntefest* (Harvest Festival) and during the festival, the Jews in Majdanek, in the Lipowa Street jail in Lublin, Trawniki, Rachów, Poniatów, and all the camps in the Lublin district, to the accompaniment of lively Strauss waltzes, had been shot into pits they had been ordered to dig and then burned together with their barracks.

A pit is dug by Budzyń's gate, above it in golden letters a sign "To Each His Own." Ukrainians stand at the doors of the barracks, weapons aimed at those inside.

At ten o'clock at night, according to Zylbersztajn, the *Kommandant*, accompanied by camp-elder Stockman, goes to the prisoners and tells them:

"It is true, that all your brothers have been shot today. The same was to have happened to you, but thanks to the efforts of the directors of the factory, you are to live. I have received an order directly from Berlin to keep you alive. You're fortunate, you are the only Jews who will survive the war. The factory expects excellent work of you in token of your gratitude. . . ."

It is not entirely clear whether the Budzyń camp survived because Heinkel needed its Jewish workforce, or whether because, as Zylbersztajn suggests, it was a ploy by certain relatives of SS dignitaries who had ensconced themselves in the Heinkel factory to avoid being sent to the Eastern Front.

Fall turns to winter. On February 15, 1944, the Budzyń Hard Labor Camp for Jews, administered by Globocnic in Lublin, turns into Concentration Camp Budzyń, affiliate of Majdanek, under Oswald Pohl's command in Berlin. The prisoners exchange their own clothing for striped concentration camp uniforms pulled off the dead of Majdanek, move out of the seven crowded, windowless, horse stables next to the settlement into forty spacious barracks with windows in the new, heavily guarded camp next to the factory. But the Soviet Army has reached Kiev and is pressing on German-occupied Poland, and just as Heinkel's workforce moves into its new quarters, the aircraft company retreats from the exposures of Budzyń, and burrows deep beneath one of Poland's national treasures—the ancient sculptures in the vast saltmines of Wieliczka, near Kraków. From Płaszów, under whose command the new camp is placed, the SS send prisoners to build barracks in the declivity behind the saltmine's imposing, clock-towered central building; pull the code-name *Abbaubetrieb Wilhelmsburg* over the Wieliczka installation for fear of detection; and between February and June distribute Budzyń's prisoners between various camps: Radom, Skarzysk Kamienny, Starachowic, Majdanek. Herszel Zancberg is sent in the first group of three hundred men to build airplanes at another out-camp of Płaszów—in Mielec—on February 19. Two months later, at the beginning of May, when the Red Army is already less than two hundred kilometers from Majdanek, Jakub, together with his fatherly protector Luksemburg, camp-elder Stockman, and other of Heinkel's chosen men, women and children, is sent to Wieliczka. With them go members of Budzyń's SS.

Again the inevitable selection. Again Jakub sees Amon Göth, his finger pointing people in this or in that direction. Again Jakub is overwhelmed with the fear that again he will be selected out as he had in Bełżyce. And indeed, the finger points him to the side of the smaller, the weaker, the older, but the instinct that had helped him survive Feix's selection kicks in now. On the point of what would send him again to death, Jakub has an out-of-body experience: watches himself sprint in the other direction, expecting at any second to hear himself being shot from behind. When he comes back to himself among the stronger, but his fatherly Luksemburg is not there.

Day in, day out in Wieliczka, Jakub is lowered with Heinkel's other *Juden* into the depths of the mines on a large open platform down a pitch-black shaft into a huge, damp, subterranean hall hollowed out of salt. Lowered before dawn, raised in the dusk of evening; dark when they go in, dark when they come out.

Jakub drills holes for rivets at a table in the dank mine whose salt walls drip water. Occasionally somebody touches an electric wire and electrocutes himself. The boy slips on wet mud and fractures his wrist—the left one with the scar he got from cutting himself on his mother's knife when he was little, the one with "KL" now tattooed on it. All else is darkness which occludes mind and memory, and silences the tongue. "I went to KZ-Wieliczka where," Pola Grinbaum-Kronisz of Bełżyce testified, "I worked for three months in the salt mine there. I was completely yellow. Later, I spent a few weeks in ZAL at Płaszów . . ."

In mid-July, prisoners are transported to Wieliczka from Płaszów and Mielec and people from Budzyń are reunited; Jakub sees Herszel again. But the transports in herald a transport out. The Russians are advancing; the conditions in the saltmines are not suited to the building of planes, Heinkel is dismantling the plant, Wieliczka is being liquidated; all but seven of the women held there are dispatched to Płaszów; and the following day the men are loaded into freight cars.

In Transit

The men from the Warsaw Ghetto and eastern Poland, who had been incarcertated for months in the desolate camps of Płaszów, Mielec, and Wieliczka, branded, beaten, broken, worked without rest, now crouch, lie, sit jostling each other, lean against the planked walls of the stifling boxcar. Some are sick, some are dying, some are dead. Some weep. Some sing to pass the time, to keep up a spirit of some sort. Some sing a Hebrew song about a train, a valley, love. They pass through towns; they stop at a siding for a while, Oswiecim/Auschwitz someone says. The name means little. Pressing his eye to a crack, Jakub sees the words "Breslau/Wroclaw" and people on the platform. People standing, walking, free in the sunlight. People in print dresses, trousers, shirts, open collars, shoes. People with hair swept back, parted, curled. People, he is sure, who are not as hungry as he. Envy overwhelms him.

Another stop. Another siding. Barking dogs; doors of boxcars crashing open; SS men legs akimbo, bayonets poised; *Los! Los! Heraus! Schnell!* Lined up in fives, the men march in the hazy heat of that August 4th morning along a road which leads out of a small town, past stuccoed rowhouses and an old Jewish cemetery in which—amazingly—the stones still stand, and then curves for six kilometers through fields and meadows, up a steep hill through the village and into the camp.

The streets of the village of Flossenbürg stand empty, as they always do when transports arrive because the SS does not allow the townspeople out at those times.

Jakub does not look around him, nor take in the faces
at the windows or the view, nor does he notice the palatinate
fort which has loomed above the village for eight hundred
years—the Flossenbürg, built to protect the Germans from
slavic threat and coopted by the Nazis as a symbol of the
"value of the greater German Reich" and as an admonish-
ment to the SS to "Remain unified and strong in the fight
for the sake of Germany." Jakub is too frightened to see.
Screamed at and pushed and beaten the column of
men is marched past the Kommandatur, through the gates,
across the Appellplatz, and into a fenced area. Two large
barn-like barracks without windows or sanitary facilities and
equipped only with triple-tiered bunks stand in this enclosure—Barracks 20 and 21, the *Zugangslager* (New Arrivals
camp). Behind them, and separated from them with barbed
wire stand the "convalescence" barracks, out of which each
morning the sick and dying—men suffering from dysentery,
typhus, tuberculosis—are driven, and off in the corner on
the escarpment above the crematorium, a large open-air
latrine, a ditch in the ground. Smoke rises from the crematorium and its assisting pyres. The sickly sweet smell of burning human flesh and the smell of human excrement flowing
from the bowels of men on the brink of death quells the
pine scent natural to the air of these mountains. In the
background, gunshots play staccato, becoming as familiar as
heartbeat, as birdsong.
Los! Los! Sofort ausziehen! (Strip immediately!)
From those last days in Bełżyce, from the months he
has spent in Budzyń, the months he has spent in Wieliczka,
Jakub has learned to read the mute language of the camps.
He has learned where to position himself in the soup line.
To stay away from the front where he might be noticed and
where the soup would be thin; to stay away from the back
where there might be no soup left; how to place his tin
container under the ladle so as not to miss a drop. He has
learned how to eat his bread: to hold it in his cupped hands
and to lower his mouth to it, so as not to lose a crumb.

When the SS walk by he knows he must not stand out, not draw attention to himself, not be seen. But now he, and the other men, are in utter darkness, stone-blind to what follows: "Strip!" "To this day," Izaak Arbus, who had arrived in the same transport from Mielec with Dr. Förster, the former head of the Red Cross in Vienna, wrote in his memoir forty years later, "it is not clear to me why the SS took away the clothing for a whole week, while the striped rags lay in the corner of the square all that time, untouched. Maybe, it was just some type of Nazi joke."

Nothing follows then, but the order *Ausziehen* that strips Jakub naked, strips from him, too, his last tangible connection with his family—the little photograph of his brother Hiluś that he has carried with him out of Bełżyce.

For the whole day, the naked men mill uncertainly, watchfully, around the enclosure. The sun burns their bodies, and after the journey, deprived of water, deprived of food, his head shaved clean of its protecting hair, Jakub's head swells and leaves an indentation when he touches it with his finger, adding fresh fear to the terror he already feels. For he has learned that edema can herald death.

Prisoners from the main camp pass along the path by the enclosure, or gather by the barbed-wire fence, and Jakub notices that a variety of letters: "P" for *Polen*; "R" for *Russer*, "F" for *Franzossen*, are stamped on the identifying triangles sewn onto their jackets. For the first time, Jakub is in a camp where not everyone is Jewish. Hope seeps through Jakub's fear. Perhaps, after all, they are not here to be killed; perhaps, he has been brought here to work!

Day gives way to evening. Evening gives way to night. The men are driven into the barracks.

Identical days in the enclosure follow identical nights in the barracks.

A group of uniformed men arrives with prisoner assistants carrying brushes, pots of paint, and clipboards. One by one, the naked men stand before them. The doctors look each one over, inspect their mouths for signs of disease, thrust pencils up their rectums to check whether they have anything hidden there, note the physical shape each man is in, dip a brush into a paint-pot, and write a number on each forehead. The assistants write notes on their pads, and then, without explaining anything, the uniformed group leaves. Everyone knows that the numbers are important, but not one of them knows what those numbers mean.

In the testimony he gave to the U.S. War Crimes team on 23 September 1947, Heinrich Schmitz, Flossenbürg camp's civilian doctor explained: "Upon arrival in the camp the prisoners were divided into four groups in the order of their strength and ability to work. Group 4 was unable to do any work. Group 3 worked only within the limits of the camp. These selections were made by physicians. People in Group 4 were placed in the [convalescence barracks]. . . . Group 3 worked within the camp carrying stone and level-ling the ground, and some specialists among them were sent to the Messerschmidt plant. Groups 1 and 2 worked in out details, or in outside camps. . . ."

Herszel Zancberg and several hundred others of the Wieliczka transport are taken away. Fourteen-year-old Jakub is left behind; Number 14086 Flossenbürg is assigned to Block 19.

Both Sides of the Wire

Flossenbürg Concentration Camp was situated on the margin of a village of the same name in the Oberpfalz mountains of Bavaria at the border with the Czech Republic. In this part of Germany, tracts of dense coniferous forest alternate with huge sweeps of bare hills and smooth valleys extending for miles to the horizon, and buffetted at all seasons of the year by the biting Oberpfalz winds. The soil in these parts is too thin to sustain crops and livestock, but the granite beneath it is of a particularly high quality, and in 1875 a local stonemason, Wilhelm Jakob, recognizing the profit that could be turned from the earth beneath his feet, established a quarry which became the villager's main source of income.

The venture was successful. A freight railroad was built connecting Jakob's stoneworks with the small town of Floss five kilometers away. Between the wars, living conditions for the workers in Flossenbürg improved. An eight-hour work day was introduced; the workers formed political and labor unions, established sports teams, built themselves a sports club, acquired a voice in local affairs, and had their representatives on the local council. Then came the depression that, causing a 75 percent unemployment rate in Germany's construction industry, hit them particularly hard. So they were pleased when—thanks in part to the good efforts of their Nazi mayor, quarry owner Christian Jacob—Heinrich Himmler and the SS determined that the village's beautiful and valuable granite would serve well for the Reich's vast building projects, and that a concentration camp placed in the seclusion of that insignificant place would be one of the principal sources of labor.

Between the end of April and the beginning of May 1938, the SS established their own company, the *Deutsche Erd-und Steinwerk* (DEST—German Earth and Stone Works)— "one of the most lethal employers of concentration camp inmates," according to the Nuremberg Trials—and, a few days later, Flossenbürg Concentration Camp, the fourth camp after Buchenwald, Dachau, and Sachsenhausen, and the fourth largest on German soil.

With attention to symbolism, the SS had ordered the camp to be constructed in a depression between hills on the northern edge of Flossenbürg, across from the ruins of the palatinate fortress, and on a slope of the southern face of the hill, the Platenberg, bounding one side of the camp, they built two streets of dark brown log cabins on massive granite foundations, in the style of Hitler's Berchtesgarten retreat, to accommodate the SS men with families. In this way, the SS with their slaves at their backs looked down onto a world spreading seemingly endlessly before them, and the villagers looked up to the SS who were to be the models for the future Germany.

German prisoners were transported from Dachau, Sachsenhausen, and Buchenwald to build the camp. These "criminals"—their status identified by green triangles sewn onto their jackets—included not only first-degree murderers, embezzlers, thieves, and so-called anti-socials, but also anti-Nazis. Among them was Carl Schrade, a large-boned Swiss-German trader in industrial diamonds, who had been arrested in Berlin and incarcerated without trial in 1934 for making disparaging remarks against National Socialism. When he first came to Flossenbürg, he worked in the quarry transporting stones and digging road-beds, was subsequently hospitalized for several months, became a clerk, then a Blockelder, and, in the last nine months of the camp's existence, the hospital's inmate administrator, its Kapo, and, unusual among the Kapos, a decent man.

In April 1945, Schrade testified to the Americans that from the beginning in Flossenbürg a "terror regime was in charge ... Germans were beaten to death by Germans." The camp's first Kommandant, forty-seven-year-old SS-*Sturmbannführer* (Major) Jacob Weiseborn, an alcoholic, and the camp's first *Schutzhaftlagerführer* (protective custody leader), and SS-Captain Hans Aumeier, a former metalworker, small in stature and as terrible as he was small, were assisted in their crimes by a staff of lower-ranking SS who, as Schrade said, "did all they could in following their leaders' orders to commit the most brutal acts on the prisoners," and "were responsible for kicking the prisoners in the stomach, hitting them at will with hard objects on the head, and were brutal in many other ways. ... They have let so much blood flow that they are the cause of an uncountable number of deaths. ..." In addition to higher and lower SS, "about twenty of [the prisoners] served members of the SS as watch dogs and created unmentionable treatment to their fellow men."

The first non-German inmates, ninety-eight Czech prisoners were brought to Flossenbürg beginning in March 1940. In January 1941, seven hundred Poles were transfered there from Auschwitz. In 1942, a thousand Russian prisoners of war were confined there in two windowless barracks. And when these foreign "political" prisoners were brought to the camp, the Germans became their Kapos and their Blockelders, severely mistreating the fellow prisoners they supervised and guarded.

The villagers saw SS guards goading prisoners down their street to various worksites. They smelled the evil smell carried by the north and east blowing winds; everyone there heard persistent gunfire from the camp, but for them, the camp was a godsend. Stonemasons, quarriers, and woodcutters found work as foremen at the camp and exemptions from military service, their particular skills making them "essential to the war effort." Some women made an income by renting rooms to the SS, as the blacksmith's widow did, who told her son when he came home on leave from the army that her tenant, SS-man Karl Hänsel, was a perfect gentleman—wouldn't let her carry coal up from the cellar, did it for her. The villagers were able to request labor from the camp to perform heavier garden jobs or carpentry around the house—a particular boon for women whose husbands and sons were away serving in the *Wehrmacht.* Young women were hired as maids by SS families, and happy to be so, as was the eighteen-year-old girl who was employed by the family of Ludwig Baumgartner, camp adjutant, because she found them kind employers who called a doctor in when she was sick, and gave her more to eat than she got at home. Many of the girls in the village formed romantic liaisons with the elegantly uniformed SS men, were photographed smiling with them on the rocks at the foot of the fortress, drank and danced with them, and married them. There was nothing any of them could say against the SS.

Over the years, the camp was enlarged. A crematorium was built to obviate the need of transporting corpses by night to the neighboring town of Selb. Half a hill cut away to make room for new barracks, the prisoners were ordered to pull wagons filled with granite and earth at a run, and beaten when they attempted to help any man who had fallen. A *Kommandatur* constructed, the boulders carried from the quarries to the building site on prisoners' backs. Three of the DEST's four quarries were closed in August 1943, and large halls built above them for the Messerschmidt airplane works, *Kommando 2004*, as it was known, now became the main user of concentration camp labor.

Over the years, the administration of the camp changed. Jacob Weiseborn committed suicide by drinking poison in his room on January 20, 1939, perhaps because he was being investigated in connection with embezzlement at Buchenwald. Thirty-eight year old SS-*Obersturmbannführer* Karl Künstler, a military man, and, like his predecessor, a drunk, took over his job. In June 1940 *Obersturmbahnnführer* Ludwig ("Lutz") Baumgartner came from Sachsenhausen to Flossenbürg with his wife Eva and their young daughter to become camp adjutant. A native of Nersingen near Kustrin, Baumgartner had been a perfume salesman before he joined the SS. Thirty-one-years-old, of average height, blonde, with slightly bulging eyes, a slightly upturned nose, and a slightly jutting chin, he was considered more intelligent than the men he served, and was a man of "absolutely no human qualities," as one of the prisoners put it. They observed that he trod very softly.

In January 1942, Hans Aumeier, who, according to one of the SS sergeants, "always took a personal part in the execution of Poles," left Flossenbürg for Auschwitz. Meanwhile, Künstler's drinking began to concern his superiors in Berlin, and when he celebrated twenty-two years of military service and the celebration got out of hand, Himmler himself warned that if "the Reich leaders would hear once more about his orgies and drinking excesses, he would lose his epaulettes and then be locked up for years." Künstler ignored the warning, drank again, was removed from office in August 1942 and sent to fight with the Prinz Eugen Battalion.

In the same month, Auschwitz's deputy *Kommandant*, thirty-nine-year-old SS-*Hauptsturmführer* Karl Fritzsch, took over as protective custody leader in Flossenbürg. An illiterate man with no formal education, he was regarded by some of his victims as one of the foulest products of Nazism, he received an SS commendation from Hitler for eight years of loyal service in February 1941, and in October that year Kommandant Höss of Auschwitz was asked by the SS-*Brigadeführer und Generalmajor* of the Waffen SS to bestow on him, "in a worthy manner and on their behalf, the *Kriegsverdienstkreuz 2. Klasse* overlayed with swords." Fritzsch walked with his legs spread wide apart, had a squeaky voice, lisped, screamed, and sounded, the prisoners thought, like a hyena. They called him *Staübchen* (dust ball).

The following month, a former baker and factory guard, Egon Zill, of Dachau, became Kommandant. "The inhuman punishments which Zill inflicted . . . were by themselves an irresponsible brutality," said Hans Maringer, a prisoner who suffered at Zill's hands in Dachau.

Most of the prisoners, men dispossessed of names and of all rights, even their own bodies, knew the SS, the booted and uniformed superior beings who told them they were not human and whose senses they offended, not by name but by physical attribute, by peculiar walk, by the color of glove on their hand, by the presence or absence of stars on their collars. And as *Kommandant* replaced *Kommandant*, and one protective custody leader followed another, the prisoners noticed the passing of each only by his failure to appear in his appointed place, his absence that day from his spot by the gate as they marched out to work, or, perhaps, one day a different arm rose and fell, a new voice screamed, *Los! Abhangen!* at executions. Each *Kommandant*, each protective custody leader, each SS man repeated and added to the crimes of the other. The prisoners dared not raise their eyes up to look at their faces for fear of being beaten or killed.

The lower-ranking SS, murderers themselves, grew critical, not of the murders their superiors required and committed, but of their lack of moral leadership, laziness, dereliction of duties, sexual misconduct, and avoidance of military service.

On February 3, 1943, they wrote to Himmler saying, "The way conditions are here it's hard to describe in letters," and suggesting that Zill could be replaced by a war invalid. With the German army retreating from Stalingrad, they, liable to be sent away from the safety of concentration camp duty either to the Eastern Front or to active duty out of Germany in Europe (as Künstler's sons' violin teacher, Waffen-SS Sergeant Max Demmel, had been when he married in the Catholic Church), their own wives by themselves at home, they had grown disenchanted with these leaders to whom, as Hitler's deputies, they had sworn allegiance, "The Herr Camp Commander," the letter continues, "wants to have evicted SS women so he can bring his own family over here despite the fact that their husbands are fighting on the front. The *Hauptsturmführer* Fritzsch only starts his duty at 8:30 a.m. and works until 2:30 p.m. and that is what those gentlemen call Duty." As for Adjutant Baumgartner, "If he as Leader can have besides his wife another woman then he's got everything he wants. SS men took a picture of him as he rode on a horse into the woods, tied the horse [to] a tree, then he stood there embracing the girl even though his wife is expecting a child. . . . We can't learn from those leaders because they can't be our example. We can only take those men who come from the front as an example but these only get mistreated by the leaders."

Had two of them, at least, not been involved themselves in running a black market in the hospital's alcohol, they might have added stealing from the Reich to their charges, since a couple of noncommissioned SS men told the Americans that one *Haupsturmführer* stole clothes, food, and prison supplies for his own use, and another used prisoners to build himself a house; that an *Oberscharführer* had run off with the camp's cash-box; and that the camp's SS doctors manufactured alcohol from the supply of glucose at the hospital.

Disillusionment with the SS appeared in the village as well at this time, hackles were raised.

Not by the constant columns of prisoners being marched up their street, even though they could see, as one of them testified to the Americans, that the prisoners "were in poor physical condition . . . some would collapse, others would try to drink water from the ditch. In all cases they were beaten till they continued in the march column."

Not by the sight of prisoners collapsing half-dead or dead on the sidewalk, the corpses being stripped, the Kapos throwing the dead and the living like offal into a horse-drawn cart.

But by social inequity.

On May 15, 1943, the farmers' wives of Flossenbürg with husbands in the army, went to the Labor Office in

Weiden and asked why the SS women could keep maids and they couldn't. On being told it wasn't their business, they wrote to Saukel, "We would like to inquire once how it comes that those SS women have still their maids, while we as farmers' wives had them taken away from us. . . . They have all their husbands here, none of them is in the frontlines —This is not right at all. It looks like just the poor people should carry the burden of the war. All these above mentioned people are SS leaders, who are supposed to be example forces . . . the men themselves swindle their way so as not to have to go to the frontlines. . . . Our husbands are getting shot on the frontline for their country to enable these women to keep their maids and their husbands home and away from the front. . . . It is really terrible that something like this exists when one thinks of the poor soldier in the front lines and then sees the conditions that exist here. If you, Herr Saukel, take no steps against it at once, we shall write to the *Führer* himself."

How, or whether, Himmler and Saukel responded to these letters is not known, but Zill was replaced in April 1943, by violent tempered, short, stocky, beefy-faced Max Koegel, a barely literate carpenter's son from Füssen, who would become Flossenbürg's last Kommandant.

Orphaned at the age of twelve, Koegel had been a shepherd, a mountain guide, a thrice-wounded First World War soldier, and a failed business man. He had spent time in jail for bankruptcy, and then was made Kommandant of Lichtenberg, Ravensbrück, and Majdanek, respectively. Max Koegel acknowledged the difficulty of the SS man's task in his dedication to the inspirational history of Flossenbürg that was his Christmas gift to his men the year he took up command: "Comrade. Remember that you have been summoned to a position by the *Führer* which calls on you to use your best manly virtues. Courage, incorruptibility, loyalty, diligence, and obedience must be demanded of you, if you want to be an SS-man in a Concentration Camp. No SS-man will be subjected to as many temptations as you. And on this Yulefest 1943, I wish you may find the strength to overcome these temptations." Meanwhile, Koegel himself sent packages of concentration camp food to the wives of Pohl and other of his Berlin superiors, and took graft from local dealers.

Baumgartner replaced Fritzsch as protective custody leader in March, 1944, running the camp with Koegel, and in May Heinrich Schmitz, a civilian doctor variously diagnosed by members of the German medical profession as a "manic-depressive," "a weak-willed, uncontrollable psychopath with a tendency to mood swings and a lack of self-awareness," "a vegetative, stigmatized psychopath with thyreotoxic symptoms," was placed in charge of the inmate hospital.

Sterilized in July 1943 and prohibited from practicing medicine, Schmitz had been given a choice of further confinement in a mental hospital or of working as a doctor in a concentration camp. "After considerable thought," the University of Munich Nervenklinik reported to the American Military Tribunal in Dachau in 1947, "he chose the latter."

An affable man, Schmitz was on good terms with the village mayor; and chatty with his inmate staff: complaining to them when there were no executions that he missed his "execution brandy"; Schmitz told the inmate clerk that the *Kommandant* had conveyed to him Himmler's order to lower the number of inmates by giving them fatal injections; argued with them about the symptoms of typhus; was fond of quips, "For sure there is a specimen of a race which must disappear," he remarked to the inmates about a seriously ill Frenchman.

A showman, Schmitz invited the SS in to watch him operate. "The Kommandant, the adjutant, and other officers smoked cigars and cigarettes as they watched Schmitz, chain-smoking cigars himself, perform," a former inmate testified in Dachau, adding "They made jokes, laughed at the patients, laughed at the doctor's antics. He, once, gave the cordon and the testicle he had cut out of one to his assistant saying: 'You can play wit this. . . .' " Schmitz deliberately allowed typhus to spread through the camp, then bragged to his inmate staff about drinking the night away with his SS higher-ups after convincing them no such sickness was there.

The inmate clerks, orderlies, doctors, and Carl Schrade attempted to temper, modify, correct, undo what Schmitz had done, or chosen not to do: they took in the sick Schmitz turned away; changed the numbers he'd written on foreheads; diluted the concentration of tuberculin; kept notes on the numbers of people he'd killed.

At 2200 hours on November 23, 1944, Höss in Oranienburg sent a special priority, secret telegram to KL-Flossenbürg: "I need by tomorrow morning notification whether existing crematorium installations suffice for the present deliveries." The pencilled response was "*Nein.*"

By fall 1944, the camp designed to hold five thousand held more than twice that number of men from all the countries Germany had occupied, adding severe overcrowding to their other sufferings and privations.

Drecksack!

Block 19, to which Jakub had been assigned, stood to the right of the gate on one side of the Appellplatz between the double-high tension fence surrounding the camp and the taller, more solidly built laundry, whose cavernous basement contained the delousing rooms and showers where, normally, prisoners were taken when they were first brought to the camp, stripped, hosed down, shaved—and often left naked on the cold stone floor all night.

Opposite Block 19, on the other side of the Apellplatz, Block One—camp office, orderly room, and campelder's quarters—where inmates were taken and beaten. Next to it, the camp kitchen, a good kommando—indoors, access to food—but from it, too, "In spite of all these privileges many . . . did not return," Emile Launois, a Belgian, detailed to work in the kitchen, wrote in his unpublished memoir, "The first to go was our Captain, the poor Ducamp . . . the Kapo noticed his deathly condition and had two Russians take him out. . . . We did not see him again."

The slopes of the enclosing hill behind these blocks were covered with tiers of identical barracks above which stood a line of dark pines and above them the sky.

Behind Block 19, more barracks; the newcomers' zone; the Russian POWs barracks with their white-washed windows; a walled-in special prison where high-ranking prisoners were interned. Some like A. Mottel, a Gaulist, in solitary confinement, others, like the Russian and Polish officers brought to Flossenbürg to be executed, held, as Mottet testified, "in cells stark naked, without towels, soap, blankets, toilet paper, heating, palliasses, very often 5, 6 or 7 in the same cell, without food or water," and where Austrian Chancellor Schuschnigg was kept with his wife and young child in a room from which, he told the Americans, "I heard the prison staff calling people forward and I heard screams."

Next to the prison was the hospital, and at the end of the little path between it and the special prison, a pretty little building with curtained window, was the *Sonderbau,* the brothel, where fourteen girls were held, brought there from Ravensbrück "on promise of freedom after six months," as one of them later said, and where as many as eighty-five men, privileged ones, summoned by a bell, lined up in the evenings. It was operated like an assembly line, camp elder Karl Matthoi, a frequent visitor, recalled, with the women in rooms numbered 1, 2, 3, and so on.

In a flat valley at the bottom of a steep drop from the main camp was the execution site where, from 1941 to 1942, Karl Künstler had groups of Poles executed daily. The men who were to be murdered were selected in groups of sixteen by native cities. Rifles slung over their shoulders, the SS walked their victims down to there, tied their hands behind their backs, and shot them.

Block 19 had been set aside for prisoners aged eight to eighteen by Kommandant Koegel because he wished to control homosexuality in the camp. It was the first barracks erected at the camp, and like all the other barracks had been built to hold 200 to 250 men. By August 1944, it held eight hundred boys. The number climbed. The barracks was dilapidated. The drainage in the area was poor and over the years the pilings on which it stood rotted. Sections of the floor periodically gave way. Windows broke and fell out. The three tiers of wooden ledges, some of them spread with disintegrating paper pallets stuffed with wood shavings, ran down both sides of a bare aisle. Five toilets and a pissoir had to serve all the boys. Four boys occupied spaces constructed for one. There were not enough blankets to cover all of them at night. There was not enough coal to heat the barn-like space. There were no cleaning materials, no soap.

"The conditions then were unbearable," one prisoner told the Dachau court. "One man would be standing on another, practically, and in the day room there were beds and so little space you could hardly move." The block, according to another elite inmate who visited it to borrow books from the Blockelder's warm private room, was the dirtiest and most disorderly of all.

It held boys many of whose parents had been shot to death or killed in the gas chambers of other camps; boys who were on the verge of death themselves; boys who did not speak each other's language; boys who did not understand German. They were supervised in Block 19 by a fifty-year-old German from Hamburg, Karl Friedrich Alois Gieselmann, former printer, advertiser, businessman, prisoner at Flossenbürg since December 1938, a swindler and a forger.

Gieselmann wore leather gloves; he carried a rubber hose; he carried a leather belt. He tore skin, cut eyes, broke bones.

After the roll call, and the distribution of the evening food, and after the boys had filed in but before they had climbed onto their section of shelf, Karl Friedrich Alois Gieselman, strode among them smoothing a heavy leather glove over his fingers, over his palm, down his wrist, as a prophylactic against his charges' subhuman flesh, a protection for his own skin, and an added weight to his hand. He walked down the aisle. Screamed *Drecksack!* Hit now one and now another small emaciated boy with full force across the head, sending him reeling several feet across the floor, and booted him in the face. The other boys in the barracks heard the crunch of skull bone.

"A young Pole came into the hospital with a thick, very thick cheek," Carl Schrade recalled. "The cheek was x-rayed and the result showed that he had a broken jaw. The wound made a five-week stay in the hospital necessary.... He said he had been kicked in the face with the shoe of Gieselman." Gieselman tore so much skin, cut so many eyes, broke so many bones that even the murderous hospital chief, Schmitz, felt the need to remind him that the hospital was not there "to repair the damage you are doing to your boys."

In winter he sent random boys—bedwetters he said they were—to sleep on the unheated washroom's wet cement floor.

Boys couldn't stop crying. Boys went mad, and each morning the children and adolescents of Block 19, like the prisoners in all the other blocks, carried out their dead.

Until he is brought to Flossenbürg, Jakub, although bereft of family, has been among people he knows, faces he recognizes, or, as the littlest one, has been protected by now this, now that, older prisoner in whom decency and tender paternalism were so deeply dyed that they could not be stripped away even though all else had been taken. Here in Flossenbürg, in Block 19, Jakub sees bigger boys, like Nikolai, a Ukranian, bullying the smaller ones. He sees that the Blockelder is a danger and not a screen between his charges and the SS, as the ones in Budzyń and Wieliczka had been, and the faint hope that has arisen in Jakub when he notices that not everyone in this camp is Jewish, drains out.

For six days of the week, at the break of day, or shortly before, in the cold of autumn and in the frigid cold of winter, Jakub marches in formation with other men across the Appellplatz, past the small peak-roofed guardhouse and climbs up a hundred some granite steps to his workplace. The fierce Oberpfalz wind bites through the rough cloth of their striped uniforms and strikes their naked flesh. The wind has always blown there, across the village, over the thin, unyielding soil of the hills of that part of the Oberpfalz, through that same quarry when it had belonged to Wilhelm Jakob, and when, in those days before the introduction of the eight-hour work day, the village men had daily put in eleven hours of work. The cold had made their hard work harder then, too, but they had not been patrolled by hostile men with canes and whips and pistols, revolvers and rifles; they had brought wood with them with which to heat their midday meals and themselves; their hands and bodies had not frozen to the stone; their clothing, although poor, had been warmer; they had worn leather vests, broad-brimmed hats or peaked caps, aprons, jackets; their feet had not been naked, had not slapped against the wooden soles of burlap topped open clogs; their bodies had not ached with the cramps of hunger; their minds had not been paralyzed with fear; their instincts not tuned to the slightest nuance of danger.

The return trip at evening is especially arduous, when, numbed with cold and exhausted beyond exhaustion, the men carry not only themselves, but also depleted comrades and dead ones back down into the camp.

Twice a day, Jakub marches that route. For the first two weeks, he marches to the quarry where he loads stones cut into sharp edged blocks by other prisoners into small wagons that other prisoners drag off and others unload. All this done at speed for eleven hours a day. He skins his fingers and fears he will die. For the next six months or so, he marches further along the same route to the Messerschmidt works where he stands at a long table drilling holes for rivets into the flaps of airplane wings, and where he and the others surreptitiously drill tiny extra holes and he imagines Messerschmidt planes falling out of the sky.

In the evenings, he stands in the Appellplatz while the strength of the camp is counted man by man, barracks by barracks. The men stand for one hour, two hours, three hours, four hours, stand long into the night until the numbers tally. They stand at attention, eyes straight ahead, trying to avoid drawing the attention of the SS striding between their rows. Sometimes as Jakub stands on the Appellplatz like this with the boys from Block 19, one particular SS-man, as haughty, rigid, and severe as the others, walks among them, stops in front of some boy, orders *"Mund aufmachen!"* and throws a sweetish, chalky tablet into his open mouth. There is nothing friendly about the SS-man's demeanour, but his action suggests that he is distinguishing between them without being malign, and that an SS man should do so Jakub finds astonishing.

Sometimes in the Appellplatz in the evenings the SS stage public hangings, and circulate among their prisoners looking straight in their faces to make sure their expressions register neither sorrow nor pain, that they are drawing the lesson that they, the SS, have power. One such hanging takes place on December 23, 1944. That Christmas, as in other years, the SS erect a Christmas tree in the yard on the SS side of the gate "which was lit up with a lot of candles," Emil Lesak, a Czech prisoner, writes in a statement in April 1945. "Two or three days before Christmas they put a wooden beam across the entrance. When the working group came from work they had to witness the hanging of six recaptured prisoners. In the meantime it got dark and the hanging prisoners were silhouetted against the light." Jakub sees the men hanged, he does not notice the tree.

Sundays, Jakub spends in the drab, gritty Appellplatz set amid the grids of dismal barracks separated by dismal narrow paths that end on all sides at the high-tension wire fence. The open space is strewn with corpses, and across it mill emaciated, filthy, stinking men every part of whose being, every one of whose instincts, are fixed, like Jakub's, on a single goal—survival. For the most part they pass each other without seeing, move around, eyes fixed on the ground, scavenging for something to eat: a forgotten blade of grass, a grain, a seed.

Some among the prisoners—the so-called *muzulmen* whom the camp has already spent, are contorted into attitudes of indifference and abandonment; they barely shuffle, crouch, sit, lie down. Still alive, they already smell like corpses. What appalls Jakub is the thought of their humanity—like his own—the thought of his kinship with these used-up men. He instinctively avoids them.

One Sunday shortly after he has been brought to the camp, he sees a man drop to the ground, his fingers curled around a crust of bread and he sees other shapes in stripes falling on him to pry that crust out of his hand, and thinks "I'd rather die than take bread from a dying man." Guided of necessity by his most primitive animal instincts, constantly on the alert for signs of danger, of possibly being beaten or shot, anxious not to miss out on any trace of food, distrustful of people he doesn't know, on his guard against turning into a *ponimaiman*, a boy who prostitutes himself for bread, he does not have the luxury of grieving for his family, thinking about life or relationships, Jakub is capable only of focusing on his own survival, and the boy who had once been convinced that his mother loved his brother more than she loved him, who had been so pleased when an SS-man in Budzyń had called him by his name and not his number instinctively searches for someone who will notice him, respond to him, affirm him, and finds such a one in Milos Kucera, in whose face he recognises, perhaps, something of Chaim.

Twenty-nine-year-old Milos Kucera from Kostalov in Czechoslovakia, had been arrested on May 28, 1942, and brought to Flossenbürg on December 12, 1942 from Dachau. At first, he had worked on the earth-digging detail, and then as *Blockeldest* (Block Clerk) and by 1944 he was camp clerk.

In a photograph taken of him looking at a bound volume during the Dachau Trial in 1946, Milos Kucera is wearing a dark double-breasted suit with a pin embossed with the Czech flag in his lapel, his hair smoothed back from his high forehead. He looks gentle and refined. As clerk, "I carried the camp files, I made up the statistics, and also carried the camp books and roll call," he testified in court. "We got daily reports about the strength [of the camp] from the hospital and . . . Department 3 gave us reports from the outside camps." He and the other clerks registered the transports brought to the camp, that on February 13, 1945 three or four thousand prisoners came from Gross Rosen, those who "were still alive we wrote down by name. The corpses, of course, couldn't speak, but we had to receive these prisoners whether dead or alive, and the dead . . . also received their numbers."

The camp office, also known as the orderly room, in which he worked was located in Block 1 directly opposite Block 19 across the Appellplatz. "Now and then, the SS block leader would come or the rapport *führer* or the camp *führer*, or various visitors would come from the outside who were accompanied by the commandant of the camp, or the commandant of the protective custody section." In this room, too, he saw the SS punish prisoners by beating them bloody with whips or hands.

His was a privileged position, and one which enabled him to know well the ways of the camp. He knew that it was Karl Fritzsch who ordered the prisoners of Block 9 to stand for three hours a day for several days; that the men had been beaten as they stood; that nobody escaped from Flossenbürg with his life. He was a friend of Carl Schrade, and, like him, used his position to help others when he could.

Milos Kucera takes notice of the small Jewish adolescent loitering near him in the Appellplatz on Sundays, and bothers to learn his name—he pronounces it "Jacob." Jakub trusts Kucera and turns to him the day in late September when he sees Herszel Zancberg, his last remaining link with his past, in the *Zugangslager* again: he has been brought back from Hersbruck, an outcamp of Flossenbürg, and does not know what is to become of him. "I'll get you out of here," Herszel hears Jakub say from the other side of the wire, and the next day when Herszel is detailed out to Kommando 2004's carpentry shop and assigned to Block 9, he tells the uncomprehending block elder that Jakub has sent him.

Jakub runs to Kucera, too, the time that, as a joke, a German prisoner signs his name on the list for the brothel, a place forbidden to Jews.

Sometime early in 1945, Milos Kucera gets Jakub assigned to the camp laundry next to Block 19. The job is desirable because the place is warm and he does not have to make the painful journey to and from work. He folds sheets with two *Prominents*, Hungarians, a former government minister and a general, one tall, one short, and learns the word *lepedö*, the Hungarian for sheets. When he makes deliveries of linen to the brothel, one of the women held there gives him bread.

Jakub now has something to give. In the evenings, Herszel brings his bowl to the door of the laundry and Jakub fills it with the soup that the two Hungarian *Prominents*, who sleep in Block One where the food is more plentiful, do not eat. Once, he is able to give Herszel a coat. Once, he gives him some shirts which Herszel gives to a German prisoner in his barracks in exchange for meat, for what looks like a drumstick.

"*Das muss man mit verstand essen,*" the German tells Herszel to appreciate what he's eating.

"What is it?"

"Cat."

Occasionally in that Appellplatz crammed with strangers: Jews and gentiles; Poles; Ukrainians; Russians; Czechs; Frenchmen—people from all the lands the Germans have occupied—doctors; hotel workers; farmers; priests; waiters; medical students; businessmen; office workers; adolescents with no formal education, all of them distorted into *Häftlinge* sad shadows of individual men, Jakub picks out the features of some man he'd known before, and those features link him, #14086, to the boy he'd been. #14088, the small boy of his own age standing forlorn in the strait between Block 19 and the laundry barracks is Chaim Arbajtman whom he had seen in Budzyń and known to be a virtuoso violinist. The man he notices one day longing for a cigarette is Rabbi Stockhammer from Warsaw who had been in the same barracks as Jakub in Budzyń and who had told him that he had known his father Chaim. And it is because Rabbi Stockhammer had known his father that Jakub trades his bread for a cigarette to give him. The camp's daily regimen, however, leaves Jakub with little room to form what might be called friendships.

For the most part, the only exchange possible between the prisoners standing at the table in the Messerschmidt factory for eleven hours is a whisper when no guard or SS man is near. So, too, in the evenings when Jakub stands to attention in the Appellplatz to be counted and recounted. The food distribution is a scramble for position in line, and the barracks he sleeps in a scramble for the washroom, the latrine, and onto the bunk and away from Gieselmann's hand. In addition, people he sees one day he no longer sees the next, either because they have fallen sick, been murdered, or transferred.

Amid the undeviating routines of the camp—the constant, unrelenting, gnawing, crippling hunger; the constant, unrelenting cruelties and murders—he lives in constant, unrelenting vigilance against death. In Flossenbürg Jakub does not, cannot, think about the past, yet something of that room perfumed with lilacs remains in the boy. Jakub, who had so carefully kept his shoes clean on Bełżyce's muddy streets, tries to avoid filth here. He draws his shirt to his mouth and rubs the rough cloth across his teeth. He tries to reach the barracks washroom before it gets too crowded to enter. He tries to clean his face in any water that he finds.

During those terrible years in Bełżyce, Jakub had looked at the world around him and had seen it in sharp relief, had been able to distinguish its features, to remember its details. In Flossenbürg where his days contract to standing, waiting, marching, working, marching, waiting, standing; where a whistle summons him to rise at five o'clock—*Drecksack!*; where he waits in a line outside in the cold and the dark for the ersatz coffee to be brought; waits outside for the work detail to be formed; marches in silence and in step towards the gate; stops by the guardhouse to be counted—*Mutzen ab!*— doffs his cap to the SS-men standing there; marches in step to work; waits in line at noon for the statutory liter of turnip soup; marches back at six o'clock to the main camp singing on command; stops by the guardhouse to be counted— *Mutzen ab!*; waits in line by the barracks to be counted; stands at attention in the parade ground; stands waiting for his two tablespoons of margarine and his small chunk of bread; gnaws it from cupped hands; files back into Block 19—*Drecksack!* His senses blur. He retains a few images from Flossenbürg in the last months of its existence: his skinned fingers carrying stones in the quarry; his hand drilling tiny extra holes into airplane wing flaps; standing with a group of adolescents at the corner of Block 19 discussing the existence or nonexistence of God; the SS-man with the pills; the woman giving him bread; Milos Kucera. The rest abstracts itself into cold, hunger, filth, stench, humiliation, fear, misery, death, corpses, sounds of gunshots, dull blows, thuds, bones breaking, a gloved hand, a scream: *Drecksack!*

Heat

Winter and early spring of 1945, are busy in Flossenbürg. By January the camp is so over-crowded that twelve hundred men, the sick, the *muzulmen,* are rounded up in front of Block 18 and those who can still walk are deported to Bergen-Belsen (the prisoners referred to such a transport as an "Ascension" because those who leave are never heard of again) those who cannot walk are taken into the laundry and dispensed with. On February 8, members of the July 1944 plot on Hitler's life—Admiral Wilhelm Canaris, Oster, Judge Sack, Dr. Hajlmar Schlacht, Dr. Theordor Strünck, General Thomas, Major General Halder are transferred from jail in the Gestapo headquarters in Berlin to the Special Prison together with Austrian Chancellor Kurt Schuschnigg, his wife, and little daughter. Auschwitz, Lublin, and Gross-Rosen drain their prisoners to Flossenbürg. On February 13, 14, 15, and 16 three to four thousand prisoners arrive from Gross-Rosen. On March 8, 1,157 more of Flossenbürg's dying are conveyed to Bergen-Belsen. On March 10, Prince Albrecht of Bavaria, his wife, eight children, and their governess are brought in and confined under guard and on concentration camp rations in two rooms of the Alte Forsthaus in the center of the village where the adjutant's lover, the DEST's secretary, lives. On March 17, an additional 870 people are transported to Bergen-Belsen. On April 1, U.S. forces cross the Werra. On April 3, the chief justice of Bavaria, Josef Müller is transferred from the Special Prison in Buchenwald with Captain Ludwig Gehre. On April 14,

Heinrich Himmler sends a telegram to the Flossenbürg command that in the event of evacuation, "No inmate must fall into the hands of the enemy alive." On April 5, U.S. forces reach Nuremberg. On April 8, Prince Albrecht and his family are moved to Dachau. On that day, too, several hundred prisoners are brought in from Brieg in Upper Silesia, all in bad condition, some have died on the journey. An hour or so later yet more concentration camp prisoners arrive. Josef Müller, who witnesses their arrival, hears an SS man scream, "*Uns interessieren keine Namen mehr, uns interessieren nur noch Zahlen!*" (Names don't interest us any more, only numbers!). That night, Dietrich von Bonhöffer and von Rabenau are hastily fetched in from Schönberg. That night Canaris, Oster, Sack, Strünck, Gehre, Rabenau, and Bonhöffer are tried. Between five and six o'clock the following morning, they are executed in the Special Prison yard. At dawn that day, the Schuschnigg family is driven away. In the same period, one thousand four hundred Czechs are brought from Brünn. On April 10, Peter Churchill and a group of British officers is brought from Sachsenhausen. The Special Prison is full so they are kept in a ward of the hospital until cells open up. On April 11, the arrivals of the first of thousands of men from Buchenwald begin. The outcamps of Flossenbürg empty back to the mother camp.

Inside the Special Prison, doors open, doors close. German voices sound out German words. Naked feet slap against the floor. Crevices and cracks in doors give glimpses of naked people, the execution yard. Groans. Screams. Shots. Stretchers. Inside the Special Prison, slits in the boards covering narrow windows yield a hillside, processions of laden stretchers, emaciated corpses spilling out onto ice.

Inside the main camp, the prisoners are ever more pressed in their barracks. Seventeen thousand men are held in a camp built for five thousand; their sparse ration grows sparser; ever more dead are carried out of the barracks in the darkness of morning; the beatings continue; the killings continue, increase. Ever more burning pyres assist the crematorium, ever more clouds of sickly smoke rain ever more human particles onto the ground. Fifteen inmate clerks in the Labor Allocation Department work throughout the day and two throughout the night picking out of the files of the living the cards of the dead. The world of the concentration camp victims—gray depression encircled by electrified wires and granite hills—is ever more desperate, and the habitual Oberpfalz winds maintain their determined course.

In the Kommandatur, in the Political Department, in the Labor Allocation Office, in the Clerk's room, in the hospital, in the Special Prison, in all the work places, the SS go on with their work.

Where there is killing to be done, there Adjutant Baumgartner can still always be found. He is seen opening the food hatch of a cell door in the prison, and shooting the man in there. He is seen ordering the beating of Russian and Polish officers before they are hanged. On the Thursday of Holy Week, he is seen in the execution yard of the prison supervising the shooting of Allied paratroopers one of whom has the name "Mary" tattooed on his arm. He is seen supervising the hanging of three women from the Polish Home Army, among them a twenty-year-old pregnant woman whose dissection afterwards he oversees in the hospital. He is seen distributing cigars, tobacco, and schnapps to his subordinates after every execution. He is seen on the path between prison and hospital summoning the corpse carrier to dispose of the dead. He is seen in the camp shooting the frail in the back. And in the evening, he returns to his stone and timber house which rests its back comfortably against the steep hill separating it from the camp crematorium huddled immediately behind, and plays with his three young children, entertains visiting SS men, tells his wife, Eva, over dinner what's going on at his work. Informs her at Easter that some high ranking German officers have to "be done away with" at the camp.

Kommandant Koegel can still be found in his office. He still raises his hand and shouts *"Los! Abhangen!"* He is a very occupied man these days. He is responsible for executions, for punishments, for starvations, the transports to Bergen-Belsen. On April 1, 1945, he visits the Schuschniggs in their cell; suggests that their child be taken away; the special prison is no place for a child, the crematorium is close by and, from it, the smell of corpses is brought by the wind. He makes courtesy calls to Prince Phillip of Hesse's cell every day. Sends word to the truck bringing special prisoners to Flossenbürg that there is no room for them there; finds that he's turned Dietrich Bonhöffer away; sends motorcycle police to correct his mistake. He receives SS-Kommissar Stawitzky, Prison Governor Gogalla, and Walter Huppenkothen of the Reich Security Office, and SS-Judge Thorbeck from Nuremberg when they are sent by order of Hitler to try Admiral Canaris and his fellow conspirators. Koegel sits as associate judge at this trial. The court is in session far into the night.

Still at their appointed places, Baumgartner and Koegel no longer own the assurance that what they are now, they will remain, and their mockery and their joking and their laughter have started to fade. Josef Müller, as he waits by the guard's hut to be returned to his cell after an interrogation one evening in April—an execution is being carried out in his prison's yard—overhears his guards remark that Adjutant Baumgartner is just leaving. He sees the adjutant and two other officers walk out of the yard. They look, he thinks, very nervous.

Koegel now gathers together the German inmates of the camp, reminds them that it is German blood which courses through their veins, gives those who will join him positions as guards and Italian mountain trooper uniforms, because he doesn't have any German ones, makes them swear, "I will be obedient to the last to Adolf Hitler."

Groups of weary men drained out of Buchenwald still continue to arrive. As usual, many of them collapse on the road leading into the camp. An SS man and ten hand-picked prisoners are sent out with a truck to gather and dispose of the dead.

Swedish Red Cross trucks are spied by the gate.

The daily roll calls do not take as long as they did.

A feeling, a sense of impending change, of end or liberation, an intuition as persistent as the Oberpfalz wind, stirs in the men in the camp.

Somehow, from somewhere, from someone, Jakub acquires three cloth identity tapes: one stamped "U" for *Ungar*, one stamped "P" for *Pölnisch*, one stamped "R" for *Russe*. He clutches them secretly to himself, these precious letters of transit, these amulets, and wonders in what order the various nationalities will be taken out of the camp.

On Sunday April 15, winter loosens its grip on spring, the sky is blue, the sun shines. A new group of men from Buchenwald reaches Flossenbürg camp, their numbers are not entered into the books. The filling out of index cards, files, reports, and statistics ceases.

The Flossenbürg command learns that armored divisions of Patton's Third Army are standing six kilometers northwest of the camp.

Kommandant Koegel receives orders from the Reichsführer.

The SS orders the Jewish patients, including a twelve-year old Polish Jewish boy whose foot has been amputated, to be taken out of the hospital.

A whisper moves between Milos Kucera and Carl Schrade that tomorrow the Jews are going to be taken out of the camp. Kucera makes arrangements, seeks out Jakub among the crowd in the Appellplatz, tells the boy to go to the boiler room beneath the laundry, that the man in there is ready for him, will show him where he should hide.

That evening Peter Churchill and his fellow officers; Josef Müller; Prince Philip of Hesse; Fabian von Schlabrendorff; Yugoslav Wing Commander Dragic; several Greek Generals and all the other Special Prisoners are driven away from the camp under SS guard crammed into a black van and two trucks.

At curfew that evening, instead of filing into Block 19, Jakub slips down into the boiler room in the basement of the laundry, crawls, as he is instructed by the German with a green triangle working there, between the thick pipes which, running beneath the Appellplatz, carry steam to laundry and kitchen. The lights burn late in the Kommandant's office that night. Max Koegel holds a meeting with his leading SS men and summons *Lagerältester*, German inmate Anton Uhl. In the Kommandant's office, stocky, florid complexioned, thick-lipped Max Koegel and heavy-set, swarthy, crooked-nosed Anton Uhl mouth words at each other. The SS, Koegel says, are leaving the camp. Tells Uhl he is free to go where he pleases. They would both, it appears, prefer to remain on the job. Uhl wishes to stick with his comrades, the inmates he's abused; Koegel to surrender the camp personally into U.S. hands, but Reichsführer Himmler commands. Max Koegel must go.

Anton Uhl goes back to his quarters in Barracks 1 and readies the camp's German inmate police force.

At dawn on Monday April 16:

Alle Juden Raus!

Alle Juden antreten!

Herszel Zancberg, Rabbi Stockhammer, and sixteen hundred other Jewish men are routed from their barracks, assembled in the Appellplatz, and, then, under guard, escorted out.

The sentries climb down from their guardtowers.

The SS leave Flossenbürg camp.

From beyond the hills, comes the sound of gun fire. U.S. planes streak the blue April sky. There is confusion now among the prisoners of Flossenbürg. Some prisoners hang white flags to attract the attention of those U.S. pilots. Some men run up to the fence, it is still electrified, they die. Some men raid the kitchens. From some of the barracks comes the sound of Russian voices singing Russian songs. Some of the prisoners mutter that this is the end. Some that this is just a trick. The German prisoners who make up the police force order the flags lowered.

Jakub lies sweltering in the suffocating heat underneath the Appellplatz, blinded by darkness. Above his head is a heavy asbestos covered pipe, beneath his back a heavy asbestos-covered pipe. He cannot stand, he cannot sit, he cannot stretch his arms out wide, he cannot raise his head, he cannot see, and his thoughts are as constrained as his body. He fears that the German with the green triangle, a man he does not know and under whose mercy he has placed himself, will denounce him, and he listens for the clatter of well-shod feet, for the kicking open of a door, more footsteps, German voices, shots. He lies and he listens for what seems to him like days in the eternal present of confinement, oppression and dread. Then, he hears footsteps, a German voice, but the voice is benign, the prisoner with the green triangle tells him the SS have left, it is safe now for him to emerge.

As usual, the dead lie scattered in the Appellplatz and along the pathways, but Jakub sees that the glass enclosures at the peak of the guardtowers are free of SS guards. The Appellplatz is crowded. He sees the U.S. planes. He feels the uncertainty, but the spring sun is shining and, for now, with the SS gone there is nothing to fear.

It was overdetermined that sunshine flaunted the vision of spring before the eyes of tortured, frozen, winter-weary wretches on the day the SS left the camp. It was over-determined that the clouds, the wind and the cold reclaimed their place as Patton's Third Army veered east and the SS returned.

Exposed in the Appellplatz of a camp which, supposedly, had been cleared of Jews, Jakub is caught in more than the mortal danger usual in the camp. Nikolai, the boy from his barracks, notices Jakub standing near him, that he has seen that boy before and realizes that Jakub is Jewish. Pointing his finger at him in disbelief, exclaims: "There still one Jew left here!"

Jakub, petrified that others have heard what the Ukrainian has said, slips out of Nikolai's line of vision, and makes his way furtively, watchfully, through the crowd searching for Milos Kucera, and tells him of his predicament. Kucera tells him to go to the hospital, find Carl Schrade and say that Milos has sent him.

Carl Schrade takes an identity tag cut from the striped jacket of a Russian who had died in the hospital out of his private cache of other such tags, instructs Vladimir, a prisoner-nurse to sew it to Jakub's jacket, then leads the boy to the typhus ward, and points out the bunk he should lie on.

"I am Vaganov, Vassily, from Kharkov; Vaganov, Vassily, from Kharkov; Vaganov, Vass . . ."

Even here in the typhus ward; the dingy, depressing ward where debilitated men, half-dead from fever, intense diarrhea, and dehydration lie one to a bunk in double tiers; even here on the ward the SS avoid; here where Carl Schrade and Vladimir, the nurse, have placed him; even here, Jakub has to be careful.

"Vaganov, Vassily," he mutters when they come around distributing the bread. A weak voice from the bunk above him echoes, "Vassily! My compatriot! Is that you?"

The poor wretched man may have just needed the comfort of a familiar voice but Jakub dare not take the chance of being exposed and he seeks out Carl Schrade again who moves him to a different bunk at the other end of the ward.

Snow and rain begin to fall across the Oberpfalz.

Back in his office once more, Kommandant Koegel plans the evacuation of the camp. In the autopark on the other side of the fence, men work without ceasing readying trucks. New reinforcements of SS men arrive at the camp. The French inmate doctors inject Sergeant Demmel in the foot with fenol so that he will be sent to a neighboring hospital instead of going as a guard on the march. Prisoners from other camps continue arriving; the weaker are shot; the path between the hospital and the special prison, the Appellplatz, and all the thoroughfares of the camp are piled higher than usual with dead and sodden with blood. The crematorium, the wooden pyres, working by night as well as by day are insufficient to burn all the dead.

The order comes down from Kommandant Koegel that all written records must be destroyed. In all the offices, in the Kommandatur as well as the camp, SS men and inmate clerks undo all the work they have done. They empty file drawers, remove registers, papers, cards. And just as when those same inmates had earlier pocketed those stencilled scraps of cloth, those identity tags, salvaged from the striped jackets of men who had died, and doctored the books and the cards in an effort to save men's lives, so now, when they are able, they take documents and hide them. Kurt Göltz, the hospital clerk, passes the hospital's death book to Carl Schrade who hides it under coal in one of the hospital's bins; Adolf Kleinman, a clerk in Block 1, saves a camp register; others place papers beneath the loose boards of a floor; the card index from the Personal Effects storeroom survives. For three days, documents burn.

The question which creeps from prisoner to prisoner is no longer whether the end is at hand, but what will happen, and how, and when?

There is commotion now in the village of Flossenbürg. The houses in the SS *Siedlung* on Ober- and Unter-Platenberg Streets are empty. The SS wives and families have scattered.

Eva Baumgartner taking only her three children, her parents from Berlin who are staying with her, and her bed-linen, has gone to the Gasthaus Blei, which squats below the level of the street in the tiny nearby hamlet of Altglashütte. Widow Blei's daughter married the son of SS-*Oberscharführer* Heinig, the man in charge of the camp's SS mess hall, and a number of SS women have taken shelter there.

The Baumgartner's maid has left her employers and returned to lesser comfort at her mother's and father's.

In the Koegel's blank-faced house, attached to that of the *Bürgermeister* on a street in the center of the village, the skulls and antlers of dead deer and elk, the plump, naked, German maidens captured in oil paints performing an ecstatic dance are gazed on by nobody now. Anna Koegel, taking only her bed-linen, is reputed to have gone with SS-*Obersturmführer* Drees to prepare accommodations in Reutte in the Tirol for the one hundred other SS wives who are heading there in buses. Her landlord, *Bürgermeister* Jakob, on the other hand, is sure she has gone back to her husband's hometown, Füssen.

Other fragments of the SS superstructure can be found dispersed among the small villages in the radius of Flossenbürg. They admit to no future plans, but they expect to reunite with their men when, what they call "the whole thing," blows over.

On the morning of April 20, 1945, Hitler's birthday, Koegel once again summons Anton Uhl, tells him that by order of the *Reichsführer*, the whole camp has to be evacuated, and that this time Uhl, too, must leave. From a neighboring office, Uhl hears Baumgartner's voice repeating Himmler's charge: "No inmate must fall into the hands of the enemy alive."

The echo of the adjutant's statement bounces from barracks to barracks.

On the morning of April 20, the poor condemned men are told to evacuate the barracks. Some take a blanket to protect themselves from the cold, the rain, and the snow. They are ordered to assemble by block. They are issued a piece of bread, or a spoonful of raw grain, and marched out in groups of several thousand, beginning at around seven in the morning. Adjutant Baumgartner commits his final murders in the emptying camp. He shoots those who, although they are still able to stand, are too weak to march, breaking his work twice to telephone his wife and tell her that he is leaving for Dachau after all the inmates have departed the camp.

The last group of men leaves Flossenbürg as darkness begins to set in. SS-man Kirsamer, hands the key to the storeroom that he has looted over the years to Carl Schrade and leaves.

The lights go out in the Kommandatur on the night of Hitler's birthday. Inside, all semblance of order has gone. In the rooms which open off the stony corridors, drawers gape open; their contents lie on floors and on desk tops: copies of a telegram assuring a family that their son and nephew is in good health and performing well at the camp; a letter from a Czech woman enclosing warm underwear and socks for her boy; three-quarter face photo-portraits of confident SS-men with death's-heads on their collars; commendations and awards given to Fritszch by Hitler; Koegel's brief life story and a canister of mustard gas.

Carrying a machine gun on his back, an ammunition belt across his chest, a pistol in his hand, Kommandant Koegel makes his final patrol. He walks across the Appell-platz, walks by the hospital, kicks closed doors open to check that no one is hiding inside. Then, he and his adjutant get into a black limousine loaded with weapons and suitcases, two of which are filled with gold and valuables they have taken from the prisoners' personal effects, hand the keys of the camp over to *Bürgermeister* Jakob, and drive away from Flossenbürg.

Jakub Szabmacher stretched out on a bunk in the ty-phus ward; the poor condemned sick men in the hospital lying helpless in their bunks; Carl Schrade; Kurt Göltz; the nurses, orderlies and prisoner doctors left behind ruminate the SS threat to return.

A Child Again

A photograph taken on May 1945 by the Signal Corps of the 97th Division of the U.S. Third Army shows two horses pulling a farmwagon with coffins out of Flossenbürg concentration camp. A large piece of white cloth with the word *Quarantäne* written on it in large letters is tacked on a frame to the right of the gate; the ears of one of the horses partly obscure the Gothic letters making up the word *Arbeit* carved on a gatepost. A procession of eight men accompanies the wagon. To the right, on the other side of the gate, stands a long, low barracks with narrow windows, and, beyond it, a taller one with what look like dormer windows and three thick, square chimneys. It is sleeting. Puddles glisten in the foreground, and the roofs of the two barracks are white. Whiteness smudges out whatever it is that lies in the distance beyond the buildings.

The small figure which can be seen in profile with his back to the open gate, the top of his head reaching only as far as the shoulders of the men walking by the coffins, is fifteen-year-old Jakub Szabmacher. He stands wearing an ill-fitting jacket with his arms by his side at what might be called attention were there any energy in his posture.

The man taking this documentary photograph accidentally also documented Jakub in the period when the numbness that has ever increasingly paralyzed him since the day in May 1943 when Reinhold Feix murdered Jews in Bełżyce is starting to dissipate. For the first time in almost two years, Jakub is driven by something other than instinct. For the first time in almost two years, images of Bluma, Dewora, Miriam, Hiluś and of Chaim can rise and be held in his mind. For the first time in almost two years, Jakub feels something other than terror. What he feels is totally alone and profoundly depressed.

Two days after the SS had marched the inmates out of the camp, Emil Lesak, typing his life story in the clerk's room, interrupted his narrative:

"The liberators are here. It is 23d April 1945 at 1050 hours. I just hung up the sign which I had ready "PRISONERS HAPPY END" WELCOME. and gave information about hidden weapons. One lieutenant and four other soldiers looked everything over."

Jakub had walked towards those Americans holding out to them in his outstretched hands the German rifle he had looted from the SS storeroom and had watched in amazement as a red-haired soldier had taken the rifle and broken it in two.

On the following day, April 24, Infantry Lieutenant Colonel W. I. Russell of the 90th Division of the U.S. Third Army distributed the following report to the CG XII Corps and to the CG 90th Infantry Division:

"There are 1,600 political prisoners at this camp, 20 criminal prisoners who have served their terms and 5 religious prisoners. These prisoners are of various nationalities of German overrun territories. They have formed a commission among themselves headed by a Swiss with each nationality group represented.

"The health of the inmates is bad. All are suffering from malnutrition. There are 186 active typhus cases, 98 cases of tuberculosis, confined to bed, 2 cases of diphtheria, 2 cases of scarlet fever and several cases of other communicable diseases. The whole place is lousy. Dusting team has been requested from Corps and Corps medical channels have been notified of contagious diseases. There is a crematory now operating for disposal of the dead.

"Food is short, however, there are stocks of potatoes on hand, and there is a limited supply of bread available in two towns near the camp. Transportation and supply of this bread will be arranged for. Starting April 24, 800 rations per day will be supplied by the Division until such time as supplies can be brought up by teams under direction of Corps. This will not exceed 3 days duration.

"The records of the camp are at the camp and available for use and inspection. All sections of higher authority, Corps, have been notified of all details pertinent to their particular interest in this matter."

The first Americans to enter Flossenbürg were front-line troops on their way to Czechoslovakia. They had passed on their way a wagon filled with bodies, some of which were moving. They had driven through the village whose inhabitants were nowhere to be seen. At the gate into the camp, a Belgian prisoner had warned them not to enter because typhus raged inside. They entered, stayed half an hour or so. Others came.

What these passers-through saw impressed itself on their memories. They saw jackets and blankets littering the sides of the road to the camp; bodies by the crematorium; a pile of shoes; a little train used to cart bodies down to the crematorium for burning; figures that lay or crawled; yellowed faces. They heard a dreadful silence, and, above all, they smelled the camp even before they saw it. "I got sick at the crematorium. I couldn't stand the stench," Major Falvey of the 90th Division said. "The whole area was strewn with parts of human bodies and there was a terrible odor," Brigadier General Sherman V. Hasbrouck, 97th Division, who stopped to inspect the area recalled the smell "not of decay but of burning human flesh." "The overpowering smell of burned flesh, shocked and stunned me," his staff surgeon, John F. Kelley said in a letter to him.

"I could not immediately comprehend all I saw," Dr. McConahey, a doctor with the 90th Division, says about his own stay of a few hours in Flossenbürg in his memoir *Battalion Surgeon*.

On April 28, a platoon of infantrymen from First Battalion, 386th Infantry, 97th Division was placed on guard in Flossenbürg; a Third Army War Crimes Investigation Team, consisting of 2nd Lieutenant John J. Reid and Tec 5 Benjamin B. Ferencz arrived and began taking statements: "*I, John J. Reid, 2d. Lt AUS Field Investigator, certify that this photograph was exhibited to inmates of the Flossenburg Concentration Camp, Germany, on 28 April 1945 and was identified by them as being . . . Ring . . . Michels . . . , Mohr . . . Strelau . . . Stendel . . . Koegel . . . Baumgartner. . . . a member of the SS Troops in charge of this camp. . . .*" On April 29, judge-advocates, an inspector-general, and a medical inspector were sent from their headquarters in Weiden to report on the situation at the camp, and photographers from the 97th Division arrived and began to take pictures: "*These are the bodies of Jewish, French, Russian and Slav forced laborers who died at Flossenbürg. . . . These four starved victims of Nazi brutality were found at the Flossenbürg Concentration Camp. . . . A French guide shows a 97th Division officer the crematory. . . .*"

On April 30, Major Samuel S. Gray, Jr. arrived there with several officers from his detachment on orders to take charge of the camp, and as all these more permanent forces started looking, listening, investigating, recording, the terse factual language of that initial report, the revulsion those first visitors felt which stifled the words they might have used to record what they saw, are replaced by animated descriptions of a palpable place and the former inmates become individuals, have personalities, names.

"When I got there it was in a state of high confusion," Captain Lawrence Salter, a medical officer who arrived at the end of April, said. "The Armored Division . . . had just been through there the day before and everybody was running around doing nothing at all except dying . . . some of them beat half to death, no skin on their asses from being flogged and a lot of them had typhus and starvation and malnutrition. . . ."

The Czech *Häftling* doctor, a specialist on typhus, who had watched with horror as Nazi Doctor Heinrich Schmitz had deliberately allowed the disease to spread through the camp, is now the chief physician at the hospital. His name is Francis Pollack. He comes from Prague, is married, has a daughter he has not seen because she was born after his arrest for disrupting one of Hitler's radio broadcasts by using his X-ray machine. He "understands just enough English to smile and say yes to almost everything I say," Gray writes to his wife, Martha, "He amused me very much yesterday. He renders the medical report every morning giving the diseases, new cases, etc. Looking down the disease column the following line-up met the eye: Surgery, Typhus, T.B., Women. I kidded him about it today."

The Russian *Häftling* who is the head of the committee the prisoners form after the SS leave is Ivanovich Ivanov, a naval captain from Leningrad. The Germans knocked out his upper teeth with a hammer and a punch.

The one American citizen imprisoned at the camp, Sylvester Kressewitsch, had been visiting his grandparents in Yugoslavia when the war broke out, was drafted into their army and captured by the Germans on June 14, 1941. He is suffering from tuberculosis and his condition is thought to be terminal.

The skeletal figure who speaks in English to Major Gray when he visits the TB ward on his arrival is Max Regnier, a Frenchman, "This morning," Major Gray writes, "he asked if he could have a little meat Saturday. It will be his daughter's seventh birthday, and he is going to save his eggs and have three or four friends in to eat an omelet."

One of the healthier inmates working at the hospital is Jean Michelin who tells Judge-Advocate Ralph W. Yarborough of the 97th Division, later U.S. Senator, that he's concerned about his father whom the Germans had taken to Ohrdruff.

Some of the Americans pluck Jakub, too, from anonymity and oblivion. Lieutenant Ivan Brook Oppenheimer, Counter Intelligence Corps, gives Jakub, the youngest inmate remaining there, the job of opening and closing the gates to the contaminated camp. In a film made by the 97th Division on the occasion of General Milton J. Halsey's inspection tour (the afternoon of the day Gray and Oppenheimer arrived), Jakub can be seen standing with his head slightly lowered peering with a reticent curiosity at the Americans.

"We found a Jewish lad of about thirteen or fourteen who had been a prisoner," Leslie A. Thompson, Protestant chaplain of the 97th Division, who came to perform burials in Flossenbürg with the Jewish chaplain, Captain Goldstein, wrote in the memoir he distributed to his congregation in 1975, "he and our Jewish chaplain spoke in Yiddish, which became our language of contact. . . . This young boy became our tour guide. He showed us one of the barracks where the prisoners stayed. He told of sleeping on the bare wooden bunks. Sometimes the person sleeping next to him had died in the night. He told us that there were prisoners marked for death by starvation, but in whom the will to live was strong, and these were eliminated by holding their heads under water. He showed us the path from the main buildings where the prisoners had to remove their clothes before walking down a number of steps into a small open area where they had placed the gallows. . . ."

And in Dr. Salter's fond recollection, #14086 Flossenbürg becomes the child from Bełżyce again: "They had this little Jewish boy about fourteen-years-old, one of the straightest arrow kids I've ever seen in my life. I don't know how the hell he stayed that way after all the unspeakable horrors that he'd been through. This little kid . . . didn't know a word of English. . . . When I first found him in the camp there, he was so miserable and all, and I felt so sorry for him."

The camp is still chaotic, confused, and threatening. The inmates are still fearful that the SS will return and kill the sick as, according to rumors, they have done in other camps. For this reason, Carl Schrade, even though he has spent eleven years in German concentration camps, refuses to leave until all the sick have been safely evacuated elsewhere. He is still there on May 27, 1945 when the last of the French inmates leave. One of the inmates writes to Major Gray, "We hope that pretty soon all the rest of the sick people will have left Flossenbürg so that even our friend and good comrade Carl Schrade, who for conscience reasons insisted to be the last up there, would be able to rejoin us in Paris."

Some of the SS do come back, are spotted in the woods with their wives. Members of the U.S. security guard, as well as six or seven Russians, endeavor to bring them in. On one occasion Captain Ivanov shoots two of them and they are hospitalized; on another occasion an SS man shoots an American sergeant and escapes. An SS man notorious for having shot a woman while raping her is killed by inmates. It takes him twelve hours to die.

Some Russians kill former camp elder, Anton Uhl, and cover his body with a boulder.

The healthier inmates are mentally and physically depleted: "While we are improving their health by better food and medical care," Major Gray says to the International Committee on May 1, "they can improve their ability to resume their lives at home by accepting responsibilities and learning to live like free men once again." And on May 3 the major writes to his wife, "The big question right now is potatoes. The inmates don't like to peel them and think the Germans ought to do it for them. No potatoes are being cooked in the kitchen right now for want of help. . . . That is the first big problem to be settled tomorrow," explaining in a note, "I wanted to encourage the prisoners to do something for themselves to foster their independence and peeling potatoes seemed a logical activity." Even the hospital staff who as prisoners had done what they could to ease their patients' lot are "not accustomed to giving much care or exercising initiative."

Both Major Gray's official report and his informal letters home reveal the extent of the difficulties he encountered in evacuating the camp:

Corpses—"People were dying at a rate of ten to fifteen a day at the end of April."

A shortage of coffins—"Since the maximum output of the Floss casketmaker was fifteen a day, it took us some time to catch up with the burials."

Typhus, filth, lice, fleas, a shortage of DDT.—"I easily imagined typhus spreading all over Europe and on investigation being traced to Flossenbürg concentration camp. . . ."

Lack of suitable accommodations for sick and healthier inmates—the main camp was contaminated; the SS barracks clear of lice "but in the greatest disorder of any section of the camp"; the DEST headquarters clean and orderly but lacking an adequate kitchen.

Disorder—"the main camp was cleaned by PWs. The fact that 250 of them worked hard for five days, and that three engineer dump trucks operating continuously were unable to complete the job of hauling the debris away, is a criterion of the size of the job."

A shortage of transportation because of the ongoing war made it difficult to evacuate people immediately and "prevented any alleviation of the local labor shortage."

Arrivals of refugees needing to be housed and fed—Russian families released from neighboring labor camps; Czech DPs instructed to come to Flossenbürg, "No one asked my consent, but I have to feed them."

Arrivals of U.S. generals and colonels on tours of inspection.

Arrivals of French officers insisting that their French comrades be allowed to leave the camp immediately.

Looting from the camp storage by Germans, DPs, and inmates leading to a further spreading of lice—"Having relieved a couple of small boys of their plunder once, I found them fully loaded a few minutes later and delivered them wailing to the *Bürgermeister*. A few Russians, slightly older, were locked up."

Looting from the hospital by some visiting French who "carried away for their personal use six radios."

A shortage of flour—"The mills aren't running. Why aren't the mills running? The Russian DPs dammed the streams to catch the fish and cut off the water."

Disputes among the inmates about the policing of the camp—"All groups but the Russian desired the [inmate] police disarmed (they had armed themselves in the period between German evacuation and American occupation) and wanted order maintained within the camp by United States soldiers. I told them that it was a very sorry state of affairs if they could not live together without having American soldiers as policemen."

"Combat used to be confused," the Major told his wife, "but it was nothing compared with this job."

But despite the difficulties, at 2:30 P.M. on May 3 the the entire village is ordered to attend the first large burial of the concentration camp's dead in the graveyard established, on General Eisenhower's orders, in the center of their village, the graves in it dug by "the entire male population of Flossenbürg augmented by twenty men of Floss who walked back and forth each day." On May 4, the first group of 169 healthier prisoners, is evacuated to Auerbach Displaced Persons Camp; by May 7 the sixty-five SS wives who, on U.S. orders, had been rounded up by the *Bürgermeister* and brought in daily to clean and clear barracks for the new hospital have completed the job and the TB patients are moved.

Fifteen-year-old Jakub does not immediately comprehend the unthreatening military men. The world to which he has belonged is not the world of these superior beings who speak a language he does not understand in a tone of voice he hasn't heard for years; whose food—chocolate, crackers, canned meat—is as different from the food he has been eating as the food of the gods is from that of humans. Uniform, outstretched hand holding a pistol, victim lying on the ground are the topographical features of Jakub's world. Ever present to his eye, they no longer register in his mind. Times without number before, Jakub has seen uniformed men killing defenseless beings. But now as he draws near to a group of prisoners who have asked one young U.S. soldier to shoot a horse so they can eat it, something in that old familiar scene shifts. The soldier turns his head away as he pulls the trigger, and Jakub is startled to see a uniformed man squeamish about killing.

Jakub still feels a *Häftling*, a *Drecksack*, expendable, contemptible, but now the American doctor whom he sometimes sees at the camp and the tall stocky lieutenant who gave him the keys speak to him in German, ask him his name, and tell him their own. A German woman comes in to the guardhouse where he sleeps to clean and make his bed. He cleans his teeth not with the edge of his jacket but with the toothbrush that the lieutenant has given him. He observes that the dead, instead of being thrown onto a heap, are being laid into coffins, placed into graves with prayers said over them ceremonially as used to happen in Bełżyce before the war. And as people leave through the gates of the camp to go home or to DP camps, realizes that he, fifteen-year-old Jakub Szabmacher, like a stray dog, has no one to go back to, nowhere to go, and he hangs around the two U.S. officers who make him feel special.

The Captain, Dr. W. Lawrence Salter from Savannah, whose "misfortune" it had been, he told his nephew years later, "to inherit this crappy little concentration camp . . . what we called a 'three-holer' because it only had three places in it that you could cremate bodies, that is, three bodies at a time," directed "the administration, supply and organization of displaced persons, concentration camp, recovered allied military personnel and prisoners of war hospital groups," according to his U.S. Army Separation Qualification Record. Weiden and Regensburg hospitals came under his jurisdiction, along with Flossenbürg to which he came several days a week. His superior officer, Colonel Louis Leland, found him to be an excellent doctor, as did the German doctors and nurses he supervised. *"Wir vermissen Sie sehr, denn Sie standen uns doch immer mit Rat und Tat zur Seite and haben wirklich sehr viel Gutes für die Kranken getan,"* one of the nurses wrote to him on September 1, 1946 ("We miss your standing by our side with advice and good deeds, and always helping the patients"). His outrage at what he found at Flossenbürg made him bring a German female pediatrician there to see what her countrymen had done, "It was a cruel thing to do," he said years later. "I was feeling cruel that day." But she, her family, and the other German doctors and nurses received packages of cigarettes, coffee, tea, and penicillin from him for several years after the end of war.

Salter gives Jakub rides in his jeep, takes him into the fields, and teaches him to shoot at targets. He feels for the boy so much that once when he is told that an SS man has been discovered in the woods, he fetches Jakub, puts him in his jeep, "I took my Luger with me . . . " he says, "and I started telling him to shoot the SS guy and then I thought it over. I started thinking, 'Now that would be a hell of a thing to put on a . . . kid, to have all that trouble tacked on him too.' So I just couldn't do it. I didn't even tell the kid what was in my mind. I'm glad I didn't." He does, however, give Jakub a .22-caliber pistol to keep and Jakub when he takes it thinks that perhaps he'll see Feix one day and then he'll shoot him.

The lieutenant, Ivan B. Oppeheimer from Pough-keepsie, had been at Buchenwald with Major Gray and it was he who had suggested when they were there "that it would be nice if we could do something for the children. Maybe there were some toys in the 'goods wagons' . . . at the railroad yard in Weimar," Gray wrote. "There were no toys . . . but there was a car full of balalaikas. It seemed that a thousand were distributed to eager, if not proficient, play-ers." "It was marvelous to see someone so human as you were," Carl Schrade wrote to Oppenheimer in 1946, and a year later on April 29, the second anniversary of Oppen-heimer's arrival at Flossenbürg, wrote again saying, "Your personability and your humanity came as a revelation to us. ...." Oppenheimer, when has to go to his detachment's headquarters in Bamberg, takes the boy along for the ride, takes him swimming, tells him somewhat unidiomatically to keep his *tukh'ess* up.

Both these men, independently of each other, and without telling Jakub, make plans for his future. Shortly before he goes on Swiss leave early in May, Captain Salter who finds Jakub "such a good kid," writes to his wife that he intends to adopt him. Lieutenant Oppenheimer takes Jakub's name off a list for a DP camp, tells the boy not to be in a hurry, perhaps something will come up, and asks Lieutenant Colonel Leland if he can do something for the boy when he comes to Flossenbürg. "Bring the boy to me," Leland says, takes one look at Jakub, decides he "can't leave him in that hell hole," and when Captain Salter returns from leave he is given the task of delivering Jakub to Lieutenant Colonel Leland at their headquarters in Erbendorf. His superior officer, the captain says, has "kidnapped the boy out from under me."

Colonel Leland puts Sergeant Lewandowski, a Polish-speaking soldier in charge of Jakub. The colonel shares his packages of food from home with him; makes enquiries about adopting Jakub in order to obtain a U.S. visa for him; and then is ordered to report in Paris. He is to be transferred to the Pacific theater of operations. On July 15, 1945, Colonel Leland takes Jakub out of Germany through a little-frequented border crossing into France.

Cover of propaganda history of Flossbürg Koegel
gave the SS as Christmas gift.

Carl Schrade.

Jakub at gate into Flossenbürg camp behind
Maj. Gray, Jr. (right) and Capt. Moundy (left). April 29, 1945.

May 1, 1945. Celebration of liberation of Flossenbürg.
Carl Schrade center.

Flossenbürg barracks, May 1945.

Guardhouse at Flossenbürg, Block 9 on right.

Lt. Col. Louis Leland.

Capt. Dr. W. Lawrence Salter.

Lt. Ivan B. Oppenheimer.

Jakub in Erbendorf with the Americans after liberation.

Milos Kucera testifying at the Flossenbürg Trial in Dachau.

Carl Schrade testifying at the Flossenbürg Trial in Dachau.

A New World

Despite being told by the Combined Displaced Persons Executive that "under existing policy there is no possibility for Lieutenant Colonel Leland to take action to send the boy to US"; and that "in due course, when Consular representatives are appointed, application should be made for an entry visa for Jacob Szabmacher in accordance with the general policy," but that "as the Polish quota is limited . . . there is, of course, the probability that no authority could be granted for a visa for a very considerable period," the colonel manages to fulfil his promise to Jakub that he will bring him to the United States. On March 12, 1946, Jakub disembarks in Norfolk, and arrives in New York the following morning to the sight of workmen hosing down the sidewalks and the smell of spring in the air.

Until a more permanent home is ready for him, Jakub stays with a large extended family, three sisters and their families, all living in close proximity to each other in Jackson Heights, and applies himself to learning English and forming links with his new world.

He looks at the books on the family's shelves, tries to spell out their titles. At school, he turns over and over in his mind until he has memorized Robert Louis Stevenson's words inscribed on the poster hanging on a window in the English department: "A word fitly spoken is like an apple of gold on a picture of silver." He learns to distinguish the nicer and not-so-nice parts of New York; its identifying features, Park Avenue, the Jamaica Race Track, Flushing Meadow Park;

the intricacies of the subways; the rules and rituals of baseball, America's national sport. Above all, he basks in the warmth of a family's life: turns to Uncle Leo for help with English; to Aunt Miriam with hygiene homework, and to Uncle Abby with math. Hears echoes of his mother's voice in the music the family listens to and plays, and learns the names of the men whose music Bluma had hummed.

In Flossenbürg, Jakub had found some comfort in Herszel Zancberg whom he had known his whole life, Rabbi Stockhammer from Warsaw who remembered his father; in Milos Kucera who saw him as a human, not a *Drecksack* or a number. When the gates of the camp opened and the realization hit that he was alone in the world, he relished the fatherly care and affection Lawrence Salter, Ivan Oppenheimer, and Louis Leland gave him, felt safe and complete at the times he was with them, as he had been once as a child with his parents, sisters, and brother. So when Uncle Leo turns to him and says, "We don't have very much, but don't feel you have to go anywhere. You are welcome to stay with us." Thrilled to be wanted, he stays.

The characteristics of the small boy in Bełżyce, the strong will, determination, politeness, and desire for love and approval, can be seen in the young man's letters which "Col. and Mrs. Leland," as Jakub called them, preserved. In those letters, also, can be traced a gradual relaxation of his tension and his delight in affection.

March 12, 1949, still in high school, he wrote to them: "Today marks the third anniversary of my arrival in the U.S. It feels as though I have been here for a much longer time; especially when I summarize all the things I have done and learned in such a relative[ly] short time. . . .

"I have been in touch with some of the boys from your brother's company. His captain is my dentist who never takes any money from me."

"School is very difficult," he wrote in November 1950, at the beginning of his first year at the Colorado School of Mines, "I have very little time for anything else besides school.

I will, therefore, use your ten dollars for something more constructive than a date." Adding that the family in New York send him clothes and food packages "and anything that I need. Here is a quote . . . 'Is there anything you need or want? Say the word and it is yours,'" and he thanks the Lelands but turns down their offer of help: "I still have a 'lot' of money and I feel that I'm much better off than many American boys that were not as unfortunate as I."

In 1951 he tells them, "I finished one year of college and feel that I have learned a great deal. The work is very hard and I find engineering more interesting as I go along; in fact, I sometimes think that I might even become a good engineer some day. I can say that my first year was a success. I got quite respectable grades. I finished a six week surveying course a week ago and started working as a surveyor one day after the final examination. . . . I don't think it is possible for me to describe to you the school I'm attending, it is unique.

"Above all, I feel very happy and I am accomplishing a lot. I feel better than I ever felt since I stepped down from the ship in Norfolk over five years ago. Do you know? I'm twenty-one already. Imagine.

"I signed up for the advanced R.O.T.C. course. I'll be a 2nd Lt. in the Combat Engineers when I graduate."

In 1953, at the beginning of his final year in college, he says, "During the course of this year, representatives from major oil companies will interview me for a job. The school has an excellent reputation for turning out good men for that field. I have a lot of confidence (not in excess though) but the old story that the doors aren't open for Jewish boys in the engineering field frightens me at times. . . . I'm also planning some day to continue studying for an advanced degree. I would like to specialize in Paleontology, perhaps under the G.I. Bill after I get out of the army."

Although he had worried that as a Jew he might not get a job in engineering, by July 1959, wearing combat boots, khakis, and a baseball hat, Jakub sits on a rocky ridge above a narrow valley in a Venezuelan jungle examining aerial photographs through a stereoscoptic lens. He is working for a subsidiary of Standard Oil of California.

In 1955, the U.S. Army had sent Jakub not to France, as he had expected, but to Germany, which he had not sought to revisit. The former *Verfluchte Jude* relished being addressed as *Herr Leutnant;* heels being clicked in deference; the freedom of Germany's concert halls, roads, and towns. But although the country and the behavior of its people had changed, and the currents of action covered his past, his own torment and that of others he had known during the war and the agony his family had experienced remained unqualified, unworn by attrition.

From the windows of the troop train taking him from Bremerhaven to the Engineer Intelligence Center in Schwetzingen the spring he arrived, he had looked out onto that remembered but unknown land, had seen German children playing in the gardens by the sides of the tracks, and the ghosts of his young cousin Imek, of the young boy shouting *"Tate! Tate! Nem mein broit,"* of the other small, murdered children of Bełżyce rose before him and he wept.

He had driven to Zürich to thank Carl Schrade for saving his life.

He had seen Flossenbürg again, this time from a different angle, when as a military geologist he had been taken on a field trip to the Oberpfalz with the *Deutsche Geologische Gesellschaft.*

The group studied the intricacies of the Flossenbürg granite; learned that the Flossenbürg massif was the youngest in the area, that its most beautiful onion-skin layers were to be found in the hill on which they were standing, the one from which the Flossenburg fortress rises, and then their German guide told them there had been a concentration camp down below during the war. *"Aber es war nicht so schlimm. . . ."* the man said, "but it wasn't so bad," adding, "not as bad as conditions in Africa today." Jakub stayed silent.

Now, as he looks at the dense rain forest vegetation of this Venezuelan valley whose mountains are composed of sedimentary formations, that other familiar topography comes back to his mind: the flatness of Budzyń, the granite of Flossenbürg. He sees fatherly Luksemburg; kindly Kucera; the swaggering Feix; Gieselman's gloved hand; the inmates piled on top of the dying man in the Appellplatz trying to pry the bread from his hand, remembers his own uncomprehending horror at the sight of what degradation does to man, decides that instead of spending his life examining and exploring the inner structure of the earth, he will go back to Colorado, study medicine, and attempt to understand humans.

From the ashes, desolations and terrors of his beginnings—unforgotten, approached, considered—Jakub builds not a prison but a new life.

Coda

Chaim Szabmacher perished in Lublin-Majdanek. Eyewitnesses to Feix's massacre of the Jews of Bełżyce report that the pit into which the people had been shot was covered with less than two feet of earth; that quicklime was thrown on top; that the earth on those graves moved and rose; that the fumes from the lime and the decomposing dead hung over Bełżyce for two weeks before the Germans, for reasons of hygiene, finally allowed the townspeople to bury them in the Jewish cemetery on the edge of town.

After the war a group of Partisans caught Mietek Skrajinski, placed a sign "I collaborated with the Germans" around his neck, took him into the village square and shot him. The mayor of Bełżyce was tried and imprisoned.

A group of Jewish men from Bełżyce tracked Mr. Goldstein down with the intention of killing him, but on learning that he had been in Bergen-Belsen decided he'd suffered enough.

District Prefect Kurt Engels was arrested in the early 1960s but committed suicide in jail before he could be brought to trial.

The mother of the young artist who lives in the Skrajinski's house where the Szabmacher's once rented rooms knows that the Jewish girl her father had sheltered in a dugout beneath the horse in their stable survived the war. She would like to see her again.

A stone set into the walls of a building in the market-square of Kazimierz Dolny is inscribed, "In Honor of Three Thousand Polish Citizens of Jewish Nationality, Former Residents of Kazimierz Dolny, Murdered by Hitlerian Occupiers During the Second World War." The wooden synagogue still stands, it serves as a cinema now. No one knows what happened to Esterka's crown.

Budzyń, today, is part of Kraśnik Fabryczny. A stone by the side of the road between Kraśnik and Urzędow commemorates the existence of the camp. The former Polish ammunitions factory which Heinkel had taken manufactures ballbearings now. Its director, Roman Wereszczynski, gladly acts as a guide to the site of the camp that stood on its fringe. The Kraśnik Regional Society regularly records the history of the Jews who lived for hundreds of years in their town in their magazine, *Regionalista*.

In the forest which separated Budzyń Hard Labor Camp for Jews from the road and the settlement, and which served the SS as execution site and burial ground, can be seen six little graves. The large sign above them reads, "To the Memory of those Murdered in this Forest in the Years 1939–45 by German Fascists." The Scouts who erected that plaque place candles each year on the graves of those children Feix murdered.

Reinhold Feix was never apprehended, although a case was brought against him. He is thought to have died in his own bed in Amberg in 1969. His son killed himself at the age of twenty-one.

Josef Leipold was sentenced to death by the Lublin District Court on November 9, 1948 and executed; Willi Heitmeyer, Feix's deputy, was sentenced to eight years in jail. Fritz Tauscher committed suicide in 1965 while in custody in Hamburg. No other member of Budzyń's SS was ever brought to justice.

The salt sculptures of Wieliczka are open to tourists again. The guides know about the existence of an aircraft factory and camp there during the war, but say they have little information about it and would like to have more.

Flossenbürg's first protective custody leader, Hans
Aumeier, was taken to Poland, tried, and executed for
the crimes he'd committed at Auschwitz. His successor at
the camp, Karl Fritszch, died in the battle for Berlin. Kommandant Karl Künstler died during the bombing of Nürn-
berg in April 1945. In 1955, Egon Zill was given a life
sentence, released after fifteen years, and died a natural
death four years later.

The car Max Koegel and Lutz Baumgartner drove out
of Flossenbürg "crashed" in Bavaria. In July 1945, the
Kommandant appeared in Schwabach at the house of one
Helene Schmidt, his wife's cousin, where Anna Koegel was
now living, saying that he was working for a farmer, and
asking to be allowed to stay overnight. He was carrying false
identification papers and going under the name of one of
his victims, "Otto Giesecke." Helene Schmidt explained to
the War Crimes Investigating Team in June 1946 why she
had allowed him to stay then and on several other occa-
sions, "It was pity for my cousin, whom I had taken to me
after she had lost everything else, to take from her those last
small rays of sunshine. After all, it was her husband, and
even though her husband had had such a position, so she
often told me, she still knew that he was not a murderer. He
had carried out his orders just like every other soldier....
Through me he shall not be betrayed."

Koegel was recognized by Bodet, one of his former
prisoners who was testifying for the prosecution at the
Flossenbürg trial, and taken into custody at eleven o'clock
on June 26, 1946, as he came out of a wood in Brunnau
leading a team of oxen. The Americans removed his shoes,
belt, and tie. Before ten on the following morning, he tore
off a piece of his undershirt and attempted to commit suicide by hanging himself from the doorknob in his cell. He
was given artificial respiration and died on the operating
table a few hours later.

Lutz Baumgartner disappeared. His wife and her parents denied all knowledge of his whereabouts. "As far as I
am concerned he is arrested in Munich with the Camp

Commander," she told the Americans. She told her children that he had died on the Eastern Front.

The SS man who sometimes put a pill into Jakub's mouth had been connected with the camp's hospital. The inmate hospital staff gave statements on his behalf to the Americans. He testified for the prosecution at the Dachau Tribunal, and turned to the French inmate doctors and nurses for help after the war when he had trouble finding work to support himself and his family.

A few of Flossenbürg's SS still live in the village or its environs, but are silent about the days they spent as masters there.

The camp's civilian doctor, Heinrich Schmitz, who had intentionally allowed typhus to spread through the camp, came down with it himself in March 1945 and was hospitalized in Weiden. He was arrested by the Americans, and in the measured statement he made on his own behalf acknowledged that "Flossenbürg was so designed as to bring about, and it did so bring about, the physical and spiritual breakdown of all its inmates," and blamed the outbreak of typhus, as well as the hospital's other ills, on SS Doctor Fischer. Schmitz was executed on November 26, 1948.

Karl Friedrich Alois Gieselman was one of the fifty-two Kapos, Block Elders, and SS men who stood trial in Dachau between June 12, 1946 and January 22, 1947 for their activities in Flossenbürg. He took the stand in his own defense because the one man "who could have testified in my behalf . . . begged me on his knees not to drag him into this trial because he wants to return to his wife and children . . . and is afraid that he would meet the same fate—he was a block leader." He described his behavior to the youths in Block 19 as "a few boxes on the ear" administered because "many boys from various countries would argue and fight among themselves," adding "a father only needs to have five sons and then it is a matter of course every week that one of them is going to get some blows." The case against him was dismissed.

In Flossenbürg in the 1960s the original wooden barracks, the *Zugangslager*, *Revier* were all torn down; the iron gates and granite pillars bearing the words *"Arbeit Macht Frei"* taken away; houses were built for Sudentenland Germans along the slopes of the hill excavated by inmates to accommodate tiers of barracks; the Kommandatur turned into low-income housing; a factory erected in the Appellplatz hiding the spot where the gallows had been. The Special Prison was kept as a museum, and its execution wall retained as a memorial to Canaris and the *Widerstand*. A small area of the camp was turned into a tree- and flower-filled graveyard, a beautiful memorial place. Former prisoners had difficulty recognizing the place which had held them. In 1999, the government of Bavaria agreed to tear down the factory, cut down the trees, uncover the foundations of barracks, and use the Kommandatur to house the museum and archives. The contours of the camp are coming back into focus again.

The train carrying Herszel Zancberg, Rabbi Stockhammer, and sixteen hundred Jews away from Flossenbürg on April 16, 1945 was strafed by U.S. planes. The Rabbi's leg was blown off, and, against his objection—"You'll need it more than I will."—Herszel made a pillow out of the jacket Jakub had given him into a pillow for the dying man's head. Herszel came to the U.S. in 1949 and turned the carpentry skills beaten into him in Flossenbürg into a successful construction business. The virtuoso violinist Chaim Arbajtman became associate concertmaster of the Philadelphia Orchestra. They and Jakub remain friends.

Jakub specialized in psychoanalysis, and evaluated and treated people who, like him, had lived through the camps and, with his colleagues, took part in groups studying survival. He was dismayed by what he discovered.

In the 1950s, the government of Chancellor Adenauer instituted *Wiedergutmachung* (legislation for camp inmates). In order to receive this restitution, compensation concentration camp victims had to prove, not simply that they had been incarcerated, but that they had been physically or mentally damaged by it. Psychiatrists in Germany attributed dysfunctions they found in survivors to be constitutional or hereditary, unconnected to the trauma of persecution. To counter them, psychiatrists in the U.S. devised the "Survivor Syndrome."

The psychiatrists who arrived at this "Syndrome" had not analyzed the people who consulted them in depth. Many of them found the stories the former inmates told too disturbing to hear and avoided in-depth analysis. Their own inability to take in or listen to what their patients were saying, they coined "the silence of the survivor." On the basis of what even H. Krystal and W. G. Niederland, the two men who formulated the syndrome, acknowledged was "a meaninglessly brief summary of the experiences," they nonetheless claimed that survivors regularly manifested a "conspiracy" of silence and reactive depression, anxiety, and guilt; they concluded, in Niederland's words, that such a syndrome was present in all survivors "regardless of the pre-morbid personality of the patient," was not "significantly influenced by previous background and individual history," and that "Without exception, all exposed to the concentration camp experience showed marked after-effects of the traumatic experiences . . . that none escaped without personality damage." Survivors who failed to produce such symptoms were accused of being "resistant to treatment."

And so human beings who had been branded and labelled, had worn numbers and letters and triangles, been turned into a grey and blue uniformed indistinguishable mass, were once again denied their individuality, categorized, degraded.

A great opportunity to learn and to understand the complexity of the human condition was lost.

Afterword: Flossenbürg? Never Heard of It

Auschwitz, Majdanek, Dachau, Buchenwald, Theresienstadt. Mentioning these places summons up familiar images and elicits a variety of associations in both individual and communal conceptions of history. They represent the system of National Socialist concentration camps and symbolize the mass murder of millions of people. This is true for public consciousness in the United States as well as Germany.

Auschwitz symbolizes the epitome of National Socialist mass murder. It has "become a symbol in which the historical importance has been superimposed on the physical topography. Time and memory have turned it into a sacred place that appears inviolable. It has become a place in the mind, an abstraction, a ghostly manifestation."[1] James E. Young is suggesting here that Auschwitz cannot speak freely and for itself. Since 1945, the place names have been given an almost stereotyped significance which has been reinforced over the years. This is due to both group-specific and comprehensive policies in the areas of remembrance and symbolism, which involve complex processes of projection, formulation, rejection, and instrumentalization of memory. Through political and academic debates, articles in the press and television reports, and also through public ceremonies of remembrance, the genocide of the National Socialists as well as the places associated with it have become a central component of our historical consciousness. These discussions about the National Socialist genocide are thus part of our daily lives. They materialize in the present. A topography of remembrance has formed itself out of the topography of terror.

However, although the names of former camps are almost omnipresent in the historical, communal, and social discourse on the Holocaust—I prefer the term "National Socialist crimes against humanity"—the mental picture formed today at the mention of places like Flossenbürg remains blurred.

"Flossenbürg? Never heard of it!"

Compared to Flossenbürg, the symbolic discourse that has developed around Auschwitz and Dachau since their liberation is totally different. All three names have their own reception history but these last two have become more or less concentration camp icons, whereas Flossenbürg has been almost completely forgotten. In addition, Dachau now has its own importance within an international youth travel-culture and is the most frequented memorial in Germany, with over a million visitors a year. Even the critical and discriminating studies by James E. Young[2] and the recently published piece of research by Harold Marcuse[3] succumb to the aura of this symbolically charged place. The fact that history, culture science, and reception history focus studies on these two locations reinforces the picture of the two places as being historically unique and possessing special features. On no account will their uniqueness and special features be disputed or relativized here. But the consequence of restricting one's view to these two concentration camp symbols is that countless other concentration and extermination camps have almost completely disappeared from the public consciousness. In these other camps, in dimensions unimaginable to us, people suffered just as much and were tortured and murdered in a bestial manner. It is a basic characteristic of National Socialist terror that it took place in innumerable locations, that in the last year of the war satellite camps of the concentration camps were to be found in every region of the German Reich, that the trail of blood of the death marches spread everywhere and that large sections of the civilian population were confronted with the wretched figures of emaciated concentration camp prisoners. The National Socialist terror and genocide, as well as German society's awareness of and participation in it, is given a more explosive significance by the fact that it was taken place in so many different locations.

But not only the topographical and social dimension of the genocide has been shifted by the postwar reception. The fact that many camps have been forgotten often means that their victims have been forgotten as well. Sometimes the fate of camp prisoners appeared less terrible because the camp itself was unknown. "Never heard of it!—It can't be that bad!"

In addition, the lack of public discussion about many former camps did not exactly promote the preservation of what remained of them or the building of memorials. At most, the affected communities or civic authorities responsible put the remains to pragmatic use or reused them. Not only Germans were responsible for this but also the Allied liberators of the camps. Countless examples, in the Flossenbürg camp among others, can be cited to substantiate this claim.

What we must concern ourselves with is not only the past of the camps, but just as much with how this past is dealt with, the changes that have taken place in our dealing with this past and the present-day importance of the crimes. One also needs to notice various "agents of memory" that pass on what people remember of the camps and also, consciously or unconsciously, "level out" these memories. In addition, the latter are embedded in a memory-culture. This is determined regionally by social framework and discourse and also in the microcosm of the local political context. These places have a different meaning for the former prisoners and victims' relatives than they have for the youngsters who now visit the memorials or for the people who live near them today. Journalists from the United States have a different view of the former camps than the relatives of a Soviet prisoner of war who was murdered there.

Such considerations indicate the "multi-layered and complex nature of these traumatic places."[4] The former concentration camps, with what remains of the original buildings, are in themselves memorials—memorials as corpus delicti—as scenes of crimes. They mark out the topography of what happened there and are surrounded by an aura of supposed authenticity. For the victims' relatives and the survivors of the concentration camps the memorials are, above all, places of mourning and cemeteries where one honours the dead. The present day residents of Dachau, Auschwitz, and Flossenbürg have made these places their home. This obvious fact, awareness of which is often missing from political and academic discourse, has a direct influence on the form of remembrance that we find there.

The former camps and memorials are by no means identical. The present architectural form of the memorials and the conceptions underlying their appearance express how each community deals with the history of the camp with which it is associated. They are embedded in both a local and regional remembrance culture that is determined by many different factors. Lying behind the appearance and design of memorials there is always a concept of remembrance that is dependent on political and social discourse and on historical demand. Places of remembrance take on a life of their own that depends on the importance ascribed to them by those who debate or write about memorials, visit them, or live near such places. Memorials on the sites of former National Socialist concentration camps reflect therefore at least three perpectives on how one deals with the crimes against humanity committed by the National Socialists. First, there is the personal and generational importance that the former prisoners and victims' relatives attribute to the sites of the former camps. Second, there is the political and social evaluation of the memorials in the respective communites. Third, the efforts of the present residents to live a normal life in these places today.

In the last few years research into the Holocaust and simultaneously, into the "instrumentalization" of its history has been on the increase. Some contemporary readers might get the impression that, as far as National Socialist genocide is concerned, everything has been researched and published. However, places like Flossenbürg remain to a large extent terra incognita. Referring to the Dachau memorial, J. E. Young said: "Ironically the historical importance of Dachau appears to have grown in proportion to its success as a memorial."[5] One should add that, on the other hand, Flossenbürg's importance has decreased. Flossenbürg Concentration Camp illustrates clearly the way in which the thematizing of the camps after 1945, and how their remains have been dealt with, have placed an euphemistic layer over the camps' concrete history. Unlike Auschwitz or Dachau, the reception of the Flossenbürg camp and the form of its memorial have minimized the camp's importance. By means of the camp's "second history" not only was the memorial marginalized but its reception was also influenced and relativized.

For more than fifty years the historical importance of the former concentration camp in Flossenbürg, with its ninety-two satellite camps covering an area of several hundred square kilometres, has been attributed little value. It has been judged more in terms of the appearance of its memorial and in accord with the de-thematization of its history in public and academic discourse. Dachau developed into an abstract symbol, a concentration camp icon, whereas Flossenbürg shrank in the perception of the general public in Germany to a "work camp for asocial elements and criminals."

"Flossenbürg?—Never heard of it!—It can't be so bad!"

Flossenbürg Concentration Camp: Stages in Its History

Beginnings

Up to the erection of the concentration camp in May 1938, Flossenbürg was a small community of just under twelve hundred inhabitants situated in eastern Bavaria directly on the border with the then First Czechoslovakian Republic. In the 1920s the whole border region was regarded as underdeveloped and backward. A raw climate, unfavorable ground conditions, a shortage of raw materials, and poor transport links had characterized the region before World War I and it was given the not very flattering name "Bavarian Siberia." Since the nineteenth century there had been numerous quarries in Flossenbürg and the majority of the male residents of Flossenbürg worked in them. However, the world economic crisis at the end of the twenties left its mark on this industry. More than half the male inhabitants lost their jobs.

When the National Socialists seized power (*Machtergreifung*) in 1933 this had two serious consequences for Flossenbürg. On the one hand the economic situation in Flossenbürg quickly changed. There was an unforeseen boom for the stone industry because the megalomaniacal architectural plans of the National Socialists meant a demand for large public buildings. The year after the *Machtergreifung* there was again full employment in the Flossenbürg quarries. Indeed, to some extent there was a lack of manpower. The improvement in the labor market was directly connected with the supply of granite for the construction of the Nazi Party rally grounds in Nuremberg, where every year in September the National Socialists staged a presentation of the German National Community (*Volksgemeinschaft*). This labor market policy meant that the National Socialists were quickly accepted in Flossenbürg, which due to its social structure was traditionally social democratic.

The Flossenbürg residents, and this brings us to the second consequence for the town, were either not aware of or were indifferent towards the fact that, at the same time, thousands of political opponents of the National Socialists disappeared in new types of institutions. Immediately after the *Machtergreifung*, which appeared to have positive consequences for the quarry workers in Flossenbürg, political opponents of the National Socialists were arrested throughout the German Reich and sent to so-called "wild concentration camps." In 1933, an old munitions factory near the town of Dachau was also used as a camp. This at first provisional camp soon developed into the permanent Dachau Concentration Camp and its structure became a "model" for more than twenty other places of murder and torture. One of these was constructed in 1938 in Flossenbürg.

From 1936 one must speak of a new generation of concentration camps. The Nazis' building plans and their policy of racial persecution led to the setting up of a whole series of new camps from 1936–37. The shortage of labor in the construction industry had increased not just in Flossenbürg but in the whole German Reich, so much so that there were fears that the extensive building program would experience problems. Faced with this situation, the leader of the SS, Heinrich Himmler—in agreement with Hitler and the Führer's favorite architect and later Armaments Minister Albert Speer—started using concentration camp prisoners in the production of building materials. As a consequence, new concentration camps were set up, including the one at Flossenbürg. In April 1938 the SS-run company "German Excavation and Quarrying Works PLC" was founded. This was responsible for organising and administering the production of building material in the new camps. Because of its rich supply of granite, Flossenbürg was a potential location and, from March 1938, there are documented discussions about the setting up of a camp there. A committee of experts, including the first commandant of Dachau and the inspector of concentration camps Theodor Eicke and SS Chief of Administration Oswald Pohl, took part in meetings of the local council in Flossenbürg. After a relatively short period of negotiation they obtained land from the Flossenbürg community and its forestry administration for an "infrastructure undertaking," which would ensure a permanent livelihood for quarry workers and stonemasons: the development of a new quarry by "criminal prisoners" in a newly constructed camp on the eastern outskirts of the town.

The building of the Flossenbürg camp and similarly, the Mauthausen, Natzweiler, and Neuengamme camps served two purposes. First, the safeguarding and expansion of SS power. The cooperation with Speer guaranteed the continuation and extension of the concentration camp system. However, for Himmler the economic reasons behind the "economization" of the camp system were peripheral. More importantly—and this was the second and decisive purpose—the growth in power due to the cooperation with Speer led to an expansion of the policy of persecution. The "struggle against political opponents" in the years after 1938 was now extended in a policy of "racial general-deterrence." So-called "malingerers," "asocial elements," "tramps," among them many gypsies, so-called "habitual criminals," numerous homosexuals, and Jehovah's Witnesses were imprisoned in large numbers in the concentration camps from 1938. In the early years this expansion of the politics of persecution on a genetic basis was also evident in the prisoners who made up the community in Flossenbürg. The persecution of Jewish citizens in the German Reich had started immediately after the Nazis came to power but was hardly reflected at all in the prison community. In the beginning the overwhelming majority consisted of other groups of prisoners.

On May 1, 1938—the National Socialist "Day of Work"—Flossenbürg Concentration Camp in northern Bavaria, near the Czech border, was officially opened as a camp for male prisoners. Two days later, on May 3, 1938, the first transport of prisoners arrived in Flossenbürg—150 prisoners from Dachau. Almost all of them were so-called "green triangles." Green alluded to the color of the prisoners' triangles used by the SS to label prisoners in the concentration camps. The triangles indicated each prisoner's status in the prison hierarchy. In the language of the camp, the "green triangles" were those defined by the National Socialists as criminals, arrested for petty offences or on the grounds of faked accusations but who to some extent would also be regarded as criminals by today's legal standards. In the camp hierarchy they were mostly at the top, occupied functionary positions in the prison community and were a means of conveying the SS terror, often cruelly, to fellow prisoners. In SS jargon Flossenbürg became the camp for "asocial elements and criminals." But this was only the beginning. Soon transports were to come to Flossenbürg from all the occupied countries of Europe. Members of the resistance, those persecuted on political and religious grounds, and, from 1944, on tens of thousands of Jewish men and women were brought to Flossenbürg or one of its satellite camps.

In the seven years of its existence Flossenbürg, with its netlike system of almost a hundred satellite camps, developed into a system of terror the importance of which is known to only a few today. Of the one hundred thousand Flossenbürg prisoners who can be named it has been proved that a third—more than thirty thousand people—did not survive.

The following history of the concentration camp will shed some light on the dimension of terror in this camp and the importance of Flossenbürg in the cosmos of National Socialist camps.

1938–40: The First Prisoners—Exploitation and Extermination in the Quarries

The first prisoners—who arrived from May 1938 from the Dachau and Buchenwald concentration camps—were involved in development projects in the camp. They erected the barracks, the administrative buildings, and the security installations. The prisoners themselves had to build their own prison. At the same time they began to work in the SS quarries. But it was hardly possible to speak of the productivity of the prisoners' work. The strict order in the camp, the constant maltreatment and torture of the prisoners, the totally inadequate food, and the extreme climate fundamentally contradicted any economic aims. The Flossenbürg quarry did indeed supply material to various building sites in the Reich, including stone for bridges at motorway construction sites, various National Socialist prestige projects such as the construction of the soldiers' hall (*Soldatenhalle*) in Berlin and also the SS center of cult worship at Wewelsburg. However, from an economic point of view, using the prisoners was totally ineffective. Uppermost in the minds of the SS was the extermination of the prisoners, not the production of building material. "Extermination through work" corresponded to the aim of the SS program and was reflected in the reality of Flossenbürg.

In the first one and a half years of its existence Flossenbürg was not an *Einweisungslager*, that is, the prisoners transported to Flossenbürg had already been interned in other concentration camps. Jewish citizens arrested in the Flossenbürg area after "The Night of Broken Glass" (*Reichskristallnacht*) on November 9, 1938, were taken to Dachau, although Flossenbürg Concentration Camp already existed. But the latter camp could not accommodate such a large number of prisoners at this time. After the completion of the initial construction work, larger transports of prisoners arrived at the camp from 1939 on. Originally planned for sixteen hundred prisoners, the camp's capacity was to be increased as early as July 1939 to three thousand, but there were delays in the construction work. From September 1939 the work was stepped up dramatically. With the invasion of Poland, a new SS division was set up in Dachau. As a result, the concentration camp there was almost completely cleared of prisoners for a period of six months. The prisoners were moved temporarily to the camps in Mauthausen, Buchenwald, and Flossenbürg. On September 27 a transport of one thousand prisoners from Dachau arrived in Flossenbürg Concentration Camp. Even for those prisoners who had been in Dachau for many years, the arrival in Flossenbürg was a shock. A prisoner's account describes the character of the camp with dreadful clarity: "The first day we were there was to give us something to think about. During the roll-call we had the opportunity to observe the Flossenbürg prisoners in the blocks opposite: emaciated poor wretches, most of them wore the green triangle but there were numerous prisoners with the black triangle of the asocial elements and every now and again the triangles indicating those likely to attempt escape and the Jehovah's Witnesses."[6] When the Dachau prisoners returned to Dachau on March 3, 1940, their number had decreased by about 10 percent. Had it not been for the relatively good physical constitution of the Dachau prisoners on arrival and the short stay in Flossenbürg itself, the number of those who fell victim to the winter of hunger and epidemics in Flossenbürg would have been markedly higher.

In the years 1940–41 Flossenbürg Concentration Camp developed more and more into a camp for Eastern European prisoners. The community of prisoners became internationalized. Opponents of the Nazi regime from the occupied countries of France and Belgium but most of all from Czechoslovakia and Poland—and from the summer of 1941, Soviet prisoners of war—were deported to Flossenbürg. In spite of constant extensions to the camp—in the end five thousand prisoners were housed there—it was never able at any time to cope with the constant intake of large numbers of new prisoners.

The death rate among prisoners increased to such an extent that in September 1940 a crematorium was built for the camp. This was soon stretched to the limits of its operating capacity. Although every day prisoners were murdered or they died as a result of their imprisonment, Flossenbürg did not have the character of an extermination camp. During the whole period of its existence, no gas chamber was built in Flossenbürg. But it was not necessary to build one. The prisoners died in large numbers as a result of the work they had to do, inadequate nourishment and provision in the camp, and the omnipresent abuse of the guards. The expression "extermination through work," which stemmed from the Nationalist Socialist terminology, described clearly the reality of the living conditions in the concentration camps. It highlights the relationship of tension between repression and extermination on the one side and the exploitation of the labor force on the other. Here human life was regarded as exploitable raw material for the manufacture of products that were important for the war effort. The value of human life was measured by the importance of the prisoners' work for the war, the status of the various groups of prisoners and how much "human material" there was available at the time.

1941–43: Specific Extermination and Expansion of Work for the Wartime Economy

In Flossenbürg, acts of specific and systematic extermination took place constantly. Between September 1941 and the early summer of 1942 at least twenty-five thousand Soviet prisoners of war—most of them officers—who were suspected of being political commissars, Jews, or "intellectuals," were either shot or given lethal injections of phenol. From a further two thousand Soviet prisoners, who during this same period were transported to Flossenbürg to work in the quarries, not even as many as a hundred survived to July 1942. The murder of the Soviet prisoners of war is terrible proof of the cooperation between SS, Gestapo, and the regular armed forces in the war of extermination against the Soviet Union and the peoples in the East.

The camp, with its cleverly worked-out system of execution facilities—there was a number of execution sites, a device for shooting prisoners through the base of the skull, devices for administering lethal injections and numerous gallows—served as a place for murdering those political opponents who came from a surrounding area of several hundred kilometers. Members of the political resistance, captured allied commandos, and people who had been doing forced labor and were then arrested, were systematically murdered in Flossenbürg. Because these people were not registered as Flossenbürg Concentration Camp prisoners, there are today no exact figures for the victims of these acts of murder.

Up to 1943 the prisoners in Flossenbürg were forced to work mainly in the quarries. After the invasion of the Soviet Union however, there was a change not only in the community of prisoners but also in the type of forced labor. People who had been arrested in the occupied countries of the East arrived at the camp. At the same time production for the war economy became increasingly more important whereas work in the quarries lost its original prominence.

Already by the end of 1942 it was planned to set up production facilities in Flossenbürg for the Messerschmidt armaments firm. By means of an increase in airplane production the National Socialist leadership hoped to overcome the Allies' command of the air. In Flossenbürg huge halls were built in which the Me109 fighter was manufactured. From February 1943 on, the majority of prisoners were put to work in armaments production. Because of the importance of this work for the war the conditions in the camp were improved for a short time. The mechanical work in this type of production required a certain degree of skill and therefore the production process was interrupted considerably when prisoners died or fell ill. The more important this work became for the war, the more problematic became the consequences of the SS terror. The physical weakness of the prisoners and the daily effects of the violence were having too much of an adverse effect on their productivity. The radical reduction in food given to prisoners in the concentration camp at the start of the war had to be partly reversed as early as the beginning of August 1940, otherwise the work in the SS firms would have been endangered. However, those who profited from the improvements in prison conditions were at the top of the camp hierarchy, such as the German prisoners and those from West European countries. For prisoners from Eastern European countries there was no change in the conditions. The death rate—as can been seen from the alarming camp statistics—hardly decreased in 1943.

1944–45: The System of Satellite Camps and the Perpetrators

When the prisoners started to work for the war economy, there was also a physical expansion of Flossenbürg Concentration Camp. From 1942 almost one hundred satellite camps linked to Flossenbürg were set up in Bavaria, Bohemia, and Saxony. Following the stagnation of the military offensive against the Soviet Union in the winter of 1941, the German economy had to be adjusted to suit a prolonged war. The requirements of the SS infrastructure outside the concentration camps, such as the construction of barracks and military hospitals for the Waffen SS also experienced fundamental changes. One of the biggest problems, the shortage of labor, was to be solved by the use of "foreign" (*Fremdvölkischer*) workers and concentration camp prisoners. In September 1942 the SS leadership agreed to armaments minister Speer's suggestion of building large numbers of satellite camps near armaments factories.

The concentration camp system spread out like a spider's web over the whole German Reich. The number of external work deployments in the camps increased slowly in the beginning, increased more quickly after the defeat at Stalingrad and reached almost astronomical proportions from March 1944 onwards. This is evident when one looks at the extension of the Flossenbürg Concentration Camp system: In 1942 there were five satellite camps, in 1943 nine, fifty-eight in 1944 and just before the end of the war in 1945, a further twenty.

This expansion of the concentration camp system was accompanied by a differentiation of the satellite camps. There were considerable differences between the groups and the numbers of prisoners, their supervision, and the type of work they did. In some large satellite camps with several thousand prisoners the conditions resembled a main camp. There was a camp structure and even a crematorium, as for example in the Flossenbürg satellite camp in Leitmeritz near Theresienstadt or Hersbruck near Nuremberg. Hersbruck and Leitmeritz were two of the most notorious satellite camps. In both camps several thousand prisoners had to work on gallery (*Stollenbau*) projects and in underground factories. More than half the prisoners brought to these places did not survive the tortures there—in each camp over eight thousand people.

Many other satellite camps were more like temporary work details. There were big differences between individual camps with regard to living conditions and the chances of survival. It all depended on the size of the detail, its importance for the war and above all, the relationship between the guards and the interests of the "employers." In the satellite camps units of the armed forces participated repeatedly in the supervision of concentration camp prisoners. For example, in the satellite camp Gundelsdorf near Kronach the guards were from the Luftwaffe. So the wretchedness of the prisoners and the exercise of terror was not something associated only with the actions of the SS. Sections of armed German troops and their allies were accomplices of the SS and interacted with them. This is a chapter in concentration camp history that has received little attention.

Like the other concentration camps, Flossenbürg was governed and guarded by its own SS unit. The terror of this "SS Death's Head Sturmbann Flossenbürg" was not confined to the main camp. It was also in charge of most of Flossenbürg's satellite camps. Whereas only a few SS men supervised the prisoners during the erection of the camp in 1938, an extensive team of guards—four thousand men and five hundred women—was formed in the years up to 1945. The female SS guards were mainly deployed in various satellite camps, although all new applicants had to complete a period of training in the main camp in Flossenbürg.

Contrary to revisionary accounts the teams of concentration camp guards were, in the early days of the regime, the nucleus of the Waffen SS. Guard duty in the camps was regarded as an important part of a political soldier's training.

The concentration camps were the "laboratories of violence" and guard duty there formed and strengthened character. During the course of World War II the elitist ideals of the SS and their training program were altered to suit the war situation. Increasingly guard duties were carried out by older men who were unsuitable for service at the front. At the same time it was common practice in the course of the war for soldiers to be transferred from combat to guard duty and vice versa. In the end non-German reserve units, for example, Ukrainians and Lithuanians, were deployed to supervise in the concentration camps. The Ukrainian mass murderer Demjaniuk, feared in the camps as "Iwan the Terrible," is also named on the personnel list of Flossenbürg guards.

Enquiring about the origin of the SS henchman and guards and gathering details about their lives is particularly informative. The results are alarming. Most of them were not in any way underprivileged. Neither can it be said that had they always had a tendency towards brutality. According to the biographies of the camp commandants at Flossenbürg, the SS guards came from the middle section of the population as it was at that time. Educated to secondary or grammar school level, they were motivated by opportunism, the desire to make a career, or by military delusions of elitism. In common with many others who committed crimes during the Nazi period, they had taken part in World War I and, as a result of experiencing career difficulties as civilians after 1918, had a negative attitude towards the Weimar Republic. But biographical similarities and peculiarites are far less decisive for an understanding of the motives of the SS leaders and guard teams than their common elitist ideals and their group identity. Their excessive views of the importance of their own existence (*Dasein*), together with belief in the superiority of their "ethnic origins" (*Volkzugehörigkeit*) and "race" (*Rasse*) promoted their sense of comradeship and helped keep them together as a group. The constant readiness to commit acts of violence was one of the most important characteristics of this group. Those who did not want to put their membership of the SS at risk had to fulfill certain expectations—and often enough they enjoyed doing so.

Writing about the motives of the perpetrators, the sociologist Wolfgang Sofsky says: "For cruelty a lack of moral sense is sufficient together with the brutalisation that comes from the daily work. The guards beat, tortured and killed, not because they had to but because they were allowed to."[7]

To return to the conditions in Flossenbürg Concentration Camp in 1944: the increased deployment of concentration camp prisoners in the armaments industry also resulted in tens of thousands of Jewish prisoners from other ghettos and camps in the East being transported to camps inside the Reich. From 1942 on, as a result of Himmler's orders, no Jew had been found in the concentration camps in the area of the prewar Reich (*alten Reichsgebiet*) because all of them had been deported to the extermination camps in the East. But for the SS leadership the necessities of war meant a short-term break with the logic of extermination. Before their planned extermination Jewish prisoners were now to do forced labor for the German war economy. From the summer of 1944 thousands of Jewish prisoners found themselves in the regions administered by Flossenbürg Concentration Camp, compared to the few hundred imprisoned there from 1938 to 1942. Most of the Jewish prisoners had been born in Poland or Hungary. They possessed a certain "value" as exploitable slave laborers because of their young age. The transport from Plasnow was followed by further transports of Jewish prisoners. From 1944 the percentage of Jews imprisoned in Flossenbürg rose to about 20 percent of the total community of prisoners. On August 4, 1944 a transport of more than two thousand six hundred Jewish youths and young men arrived in Flossenbürg from Plaszow Concentration Camp. One of them was Jakub Szabmacher.

With the setting up of the satellite camps there were also female prisoners in the areas admininstered by Flossenbürg Concentration Camp. In thirty of the ninety-two satellite camps controlled and supervised by Flossenbürg, there were sixteen thousand women and young girls, many of them Jews.

1945: The Last Phase—Death Marches and Liberation

In Flossenbürg itself at the end of 1944 there were over eight thousand prisoners in the completely overcrowded camp barracks. They were mostly from Poland, the Soviet Union, Czechoslovakia, Belgium, France and Germany. More than five thousand of them were deployed in the production of Me109 fighter planes. A report on numbers, a so-called *Stärkemeldung*, from the Flossenbürg camp commandant dated February 28, 1945, indicates that more than fifteen thousand people were housed in the most cramped conditions. In the camp cosmos of Flossenbürg Concentration Camp there were at this time more than fifty-two thousand imprisoned men and women. Over thirty-seven thousand of these were in the satellite camps.

Now there were daily transports to Flossenbürg from the concentration camps at Auschwitz, Buchenwald, and other camps. Already by the summer of 1944 the first of the large concentration camps in the East were shut down in the face of the advancing Allied liberators. Some of the prisoners who were still alive were "evacuated" inland by rail but large numbers of them made the journey on foot. Many of the routes taken from the closed camps led to Flossenbürg.

Because of its geographical location Flossenbürg was one of the last surviving camps in the concentration camp system of the National Socialists. It served as a reception camp for thousands of prisoners pushed south by the advancing Allies. No prisoner was to be found alive by the liberators. In the camps the executions were stepped up. Facing imminent defeat, the National Socialist leadership wanted as many critics of the regime and members of the resistance as possible to die with them.

April 9, 1945 marked a further chapter in the notorious history of Flossenbürg. In the early hours of the morning a group of high-ranking members of the "20 July" resistance group that had planned to assassinate Hitler in 1944 were murdered in Flossenbürg. Following a pseudo-trial, during which the prisoners were repeatedly mishandled and tortured, Admiral Wilhelm Canaris, the former head of the German Military Intelligence Organization (*Abwehr*), Hans Oster, the leader of the resistance group, Pastor Dietrich Bonhoeffer, and four other officers were hanged in the yard of the detention barrack. Immediately afterwards their bodies were burned in the crematorium and the ashes, like those of thousands of other prisoners, tipped into a hollow behind the crematorium.

Shortly afterwards, the guards began to shut down the camp. They tried to remove all traces of their acts of murder. The gallows and the devices for shooting prisoners through the base of the skull were dismantled and the blood-soaked wall used by the firing squad was hastily covered with whitewash. Pyres piled with dead prisoners and files from the camp commandant's headquarters burned for days on end. The index containing the names of all SS personnel, which had been transferred at the beginning of 1945 from Oranienburg to Flossenbürg, went up in flames.

On April 16 a transport of about one thousand seven hundred Jewish prisoners left Flossenbürg for Dachau—the camp which was furthest from the U.S. forces. At the same time the satellite camps began to be evacuated. Without food and adequate clothing, well over ten thousand emaciated and exhausted prisoners were driven south. In several columns these death marches crossed through Bavarian villages. Innumerable prisoners died from exhaustion. Others were shot or beaten because they attempted to escape or were too exhausted to continue. A special detachment of prisoners was made to bury the bodies in makeshift shallow graves. After the war over five thousand dead were discovered along the routes taken by the death marches.

When the 90th Infantry Division of the U.S. Army reached the camp on April 23, 1945 the soldiers found only about one thousand five hundred prisoners, most of them sick, who had been left behind by the fleeing guards.[8] One of these prisoners was the youth Jakub Szabmacher. Many of those who were sick only survived for a few hours or days after the liberation. In the weeks following, over one hundred former concentration camp prisoners died as a result of their period of imprisonment.

Flossenbürg Concentration Camp—Conclusions

As in almost all the concentration camps of the new generation from 1936 onwards, the first prisoners were so-called "green triangles" or "criminals." On the one hand, these included professional criminals and people who had committed serious crimes and, on the other, people who had come into conflict with the National Socialist State because they had committed minor offenses. Since the autumn of 1939 and to a greater extent after the end of the construction phase in the camp sites in 1940, German political prisoners from Dachau and Sachsenhausen came to Flossenbürg. Soon this group of "political prisoners" made up a third of the community of those imprisoned in Flossenbürg. The privileged "criminal green triangles" held the most important positions in the hierarchy of prisoners. Many of them complied with the SS and became their henchmen (*Kapos*). Such a camp system had already been tried out in Dachau. There was a method behind it: The "green" Kapos became an instrument of terror to be used against the other prisoners. This was supposed to prevent bonds of solidarity forming among prisoners, destroy their individuality, remove any privacy from their lives, and generate an environment of constant persecution and extermination. However, not all the green triangles were criminals who mishandled and persecuted their fellow prisoners. Some showed solidarity with their weaker and more underprivileged fellow sufferers.

In 1943 over four thousand people were imprisoned in the camp, mainly foreign political prisoners—most of them Poles and Soviet prisoners of war. There was a small percentage of Jewish prisoners in Flossenbürg up to 1944. Large numbers of Jewish prisoners only began to be deported to Flossenbürg and its satellite camps with the deportation of Hungarian Jews and the increased deployment of concentration camp prisoners in industries that were important for the war economy. At the same time a total of about sixteen thousand women prisoners were brought into the Flossenbürg camp system, which up to then had housed only men. Of the forty-five thousand prisoners in the Flossenbürg system directly prior to the liberation 20 percent were Jews.

Between 1938 and 1945 a total of more than one hundred thousand people were imprisoned in Flossenbürg and its satellite camps.

It can be proved that about three thousand people were deliberately killed or died as a result of the catastrophic living conditions. But because the transports arriving in Flossenbürg in the final phase of the camp's history were not registered and also due to the fact that the prisoner numbers of those who died were sometimes given to new prisoners, it will never be possible to arrive at exact figures for the number of victims. The death rate in Flossenbürg Concentration Camp indicates that a third of the people imprisoned there died. Exactly the same number died in Dachau Concentration Camp. But in proportion to the total number of prisoners held in the respective camps, the number of those who were murdered in Flossenbürg or died there as a result of the living conditions is twice as high as Dachau. Faced with the death of more than thirty thousand people it may appear obscene to approach such matters like a bookkeeper with a balance sheet. But it does make clear the character of Flossenbürg Concentration Camp, which to this day is not perceived by the public to be what it was: one of the most terrible concentration camps in the German Reich.

A History of Forgetting: Flossenbürg Concentration Camp after 1945

Discovering the atrocities. On April 23, 1945 at 10:45 a motorized patrol of the 358th Infantry Regiment of the 90th Infantry Division of the Third Army reached Flossenbürg Concentration Camp.[8] Despite the shock expressed in the accounts of the soldiers who liberated the camp, the liberation itself was far less sensational when seen from the perpective of the previous discoveries in Wöbbelin, Ohrdruf, Thekla, and Buchenwald, or the liberation of Dachau six days later. The huge camp complex in Flossenbürg was mostly empty. About one thousand six hundred critically ill prisoners who were incapable of marching had been left behind by the SS. Over one hundred of them died before the camp was liberated by the U.S. Army. Thousands of prisoners were at this time in SS hands south of Flossenbürg, between the Bavarian Forest and the Bavarian Alps. Thus, April 23 symbolizes the day on which the physical Flossenbürg was discovered and liberated, not the liberation of the majority of the camp's prisoners. This had a direct effect on the perception of the camp by the Allies. Internationally it shaped to the same extent the public thematization of the camp.

The first international press report on Flossenbürg Concentration Camp appeared on April 24, 1945 in the Chicago Herald, a day after the liberation. An article appeared under the section titled "Nazi Atrocities; Millions Die in Murder Factories," listing on a whole page atrocities committed by the Germans. Just one paragraph was devoted to the freed prisoners (numbering just under one thousand five hundred) in Flossenbürg. They were of little consequence on a page full of figures on the victims of the atrocities. A few days later there were articles in the *Washington Post* and the *New York Herald-Tribune*. The liberation of Flossenbürg paled quickly alongside reports about atrocities discovered in other places. From April 30, 1945 articles and commentaries on the liberation of Dachau dominated international reporting. The visit to Buchenwald by a delegation of British and U.S. members of parliament captured the attention of the press. The same was true of the return of U.S. newspaper publishers who had visited Buchenwald and Dachau at the beginning of May 1945. The visits of these two groups give an insight into how historical conceptions emerge. Buchenwald was the first concentration camp to be freed by U.S. units. It is in this respect that the camp's outstanding symbolic value—in the random chronology of liberation, for the Allies' war strategy and in the communication of this strategy in the press—is to be seen. Second, those who freed Buchenwald and Dachau were confronted with innumerable piles of corpses and thousands of emaciated prisoners who were little more than skeletons. The effect of the distressing scenes witnessed by the soldiers was increased when they were presented in the media. Whereas the almost empty Flossenbürg had the appearance of a ghost town, the horrifying scenes from other camps were clearer and more powerful. The corpses found in Flossenbürg, as well as the one thousand five hundred liberated prisoners, were only a further footnote in the chronology of earlier and later atrocities. Also, Dachau near Munich and Buchenwald near Weimar were easier for international delegations to reach than the remote Flossenbürg. After only one week Flossenbürg Concentration Camp disappeared almost completely from the consciousness of the international public.

Viewing the atrocities. While the American press was reporting other atrocities committed elsewhere, the U.S. units in Flossenbürg were occupied with pressing problems of a practical nature. Just under 1,500 Flossenbürg prisoners were liberated but on the day they were freed, 186 were suffering from typhus and 98 from tuberculosis. Many other prisoners were also suffering from other illnesses. In the days that followed more and more prisoners fell ill. On

May 1, 1945 Major Samuel Gray, who in the meantime had
been made commanding officer of the Flossenbürg military government, registered 699 sick prisoners for treatment by medical teams of the 97th Infantry Division that
had been summoned to Flossenbürg.[9] Daily, prisoners died
as a result of their former imprisonment. For the military
authorities there was the pressing question of how to bury
the increasing number of dead quickly and hygienically.
Up until April 25, 1945 the camp crematorium was put
into operation again and the bodies were cremated there.
But after protests from surviving prisoners Major Gray
stopped the cremations and ordered that the dead be
buried in the middle of Flossenbürg during a funeral service in their honour on May 3, 1945.[10] The residents of
Flossenbürg were made to lay out a cemetery in an open
area opposite the forester's house for those prisoners who
had died after the liberation.

In the days prior to the service coffins and wooden
crosses were made in the joiner's workshop in Flossenbürg.
All Flossenbürg residents were obliged to take part in the
ceremony. On May 3 a funeral procession with decorated
horse- and oxen-drawn carriages—which the local farmers
had to provide—crossed the roll call area of the liberated
camp and went past the two village churches to the place of
burial. "Viewing the atrocities became a type of ritual, a
social exorcism in occupied Germany."[11] The residents were
confronted with the dead. The bodies were taken to the
cemetery before the eyes of the German civilian population
and given an honorable burial.

The cemetery, which still exists today, was the first
memorial to the victims of Flossenbürg Concentration Camp.
Faced with the practical necessity of burying the prisoners
who had died after the liberation, the Americans—under
pressure from the camp survivors—created a sacred place
that showed respect for the dead. On the individual graves
there were wooden crosses or stars of David bearing the
names of the deceased and their dates of death. The graves

made reference to the concrete identity of those who died, not to the historical context of their death. Allthough the burial ceremony made general references to the fate and identity of all the Flossenbürg Concentration Camp victims, the actual symbolism of the memorials for the dead were clearly religious. There was no reference at all to Flossenbürg Concentration Camp.

Practical Use of the Prison Area: Prisoner of War Enclosure. The way in which the grounds of the former camp were dealt with was totally different. By June 1945 all the former prisoners had been removed from the liberated camp. Because the U.S. Army found it to be in good working order, it could be immediately used by the government of the occupying forces. The use of the former concentration camps by the Allies is linked to the early period of U.S. denazification policy. From July 1945 the area of the camp that had formally housed prisoners was used as a prisoner of war camp for members of the SS. In the former Flossenbürg Concentration Camp the "PWE (Prisoner of War Enclosure) 422" was set up. The camp architecture was valued for its functional efficiency, not its historical importance.

Of course—and one only mentions this here for the sake of completeness—conditions in the prisoner of war camp were fundamentally different from those in the concentration camp. The camp buildings were reused but the conditions governing their use were totally different. In a directive from Supreme Headquarters Allied Expeditionary Force, dated April 13, 1945, a special ruling stated that members of the Waffen SS were to be kept as prisoners of war in special camps pending war crimes investigations. As a result prisoner of war camps were set up, mostly for members of the Waffen SS. One of these camps was PWE 422. That the penal system was one legitimized by international law can be seen from the fact that the prisoners could regularly attend church services. They were even allowed to convert a barracks into a theatre.

Polish Displaced Persons Camp and the Creation of a Christian Remembrance Area. In the month after the prisoner of war camp was shut down in March 1946, the camp became the "Polish DP Camp Flossenbürg." On April 24, 937 non-Jewish displaced persons of Polish nationality reached Flossenbürg, followed by a further 1,163 on April 27. They were also housed in the barracks of the former concentration camp. The two thousand one hundred DPs had been brought to Flossenbürg from five camps in the U.S. occupation zone in Austria with the intention of repatriating them.

Due to the fact that the historical site of the concentration camp was no longer used for imprisonment but as a transit camp for displaced persons, the appearance of the camp area changed. The DP camp residents and the UNRRA (United Nations Relief and Rehabilitation Administration) made efforts to create an atmosphere that was civil and decent. The barbed wire and the fence posts—that still gave one the impression of a former concentration camp—were systematically removed, measures were taken to brighten up the buildings and there was even a competition for the best barrack garden.

The non-Jewish Poles in the DP camp, who had never been prisoners in Flossenbürg Concentration Camp, are interesting for another reason. In the autumn of 1946 they constructed the first large Flossenburg Concentration Camp memorial. It still characterizes to some extent the appearance of the camp site today. However, this memorial only encompassed a small part of the former camp area because the latter was still being used to house the DPs. The priorities of the memorial committee were the building of a Christian chapel of remembrance and a memorial complex in a valley beneath the former concentration camp in the so-called "Valley of Death."[12] The central element in the memorial design was the former crematorium. From the point of view of its structural content, the memorial concept clearly endowed the concentration camp dead with a Christian significance. In a restricted space, there was a highly intense symbolic representation and interpretation of the camp "victims." The crematorium was a relic that lent an aura to the complex. It was located in the lowest part of the memorial area and one had to descend in order to visit it. It pointed to the historical reality of the place and the memory of what had happened there. After passing an area which uses ideas from landscape architecture—a zone of dignity (*Würdezone*) with symbolic national memorial slabs and a "pyramid of ashes"—one reaches, by acending a steep path, the chapel of remembrance "Jesus in the Dungeon." This dominates the complex. The predetermined route corresponds structurally to a Christian path of redemption, a way of the cross. From the depths of the "Valley of Death" the visitor climbs to the chapel of atonement. A surviving watchtower of the former concentration camp has been added as a bell tower and this is crowned by a one-and-a-half-meter–high cross. The inclusion of the cross was not just a consequence of the fact that the memorial committee was dominated by Poles. It was to be found in other former concentration camps. As a symbol it is seen everywhere in Christian culture and is therefore part of the symbolism of most nations. As a minimal concession to the Jewish prisoners, who after all accounted for 20 percent of Flossenbürg Concentration Camp prisoners in 1945, a remembrance stone was placed away from the chapel near the ramp to the crematorium.

However, this could not relativize the obvious Christian significance that had been given to the complex. The complex as a whole was characterized by Christian religiosity and historical decontextualization and in its symbolic form "levelled out" all the historical events in Flossenbürg Concentration Camp. Despite the problematic nature and the present day criticism of the way in which this Christian memorial is dedicated to the dead prisoners, one must emphasize that the construction of this Flossenbürg memorial made it the first and oldest concentration camp memorial in Germany!

Using the Remains of the Camp to Modernize the Flossenbürg Site. After the UNRRA camp was shut down in October 1947, the stone buildings in the camp and the now largely converted barracks were once again occupied, this time by refugees from the former German territories east of the Oder-Neisse line, from Silesia, East Prussia, and the Sudetenland. Most of the wooden barracks had been pulled down by the mid-1950s and so only the stone buildings were used to provide accommodation. At the end of the 1950s the Flossenbürg municipality bought the camp grounds from the state of Bavaria, the latter having held the area in trust for the military government. However, the memorial complex was excluded from the sale and remained under national and international protection. At this point one must emphasize once again that although Flossenbürg was indeed the first memorial in Germany, the memorial itself covered an area of less than 5 percent of the former concentration camp.

Following the sale of the former camp grounds, the barracks were pulled down. The terraces on which they had been built were divided into small plots and sold to the refugees who had until then been living in the barracks. As part of a residential building program, houses were built on a large part of the former concentration camp grounds. Since the postwar period the former camp kitchen and laundry, as well as the roll-call area between these two buildings, had been put to commercial use and continually developed. The former SS canteen, which had functioned as a cinema after 1945, has been run as a restaurant since 1950. The whole of the quarry area, together with the barracks and the industrial buildings, had been leased to the "Oberpfälzer Stone Industry" a trade union-owned company. The concentration camp quarry is still being worked but has now been taken over by a private firm. Most of the former Flossenbürg Concentration Camp site is used for private or commercial purposes.

The infrastructure created by the SS, which had given peripheral Flossenbürg a massive push in the direction of modernization, continued to be used in a consistent manner. The development of the Flossenbürg that existed outside the camp involved the utilization of the former camp grounds. The pragmatic, secular use of the site, which began immediately after the liberation, continues to this day. The land and the buildings there have always served the most varied collection of interests.

Flossenbürg Concentration Camp and Memorial: Gaining and Changing Status. For more than ten years the Flossenbürg memorial consisted of a small Christian memorial complex, situated some way from the actual concentration camp. At the end of the 1950s the first extension to the memorial took place. This came about as the result of exhumations carried out on a large scale along the routes of the death marches on the initiative of the French government. Attempts were made to identify the dead and bring the French victims back to France. For the remains of most of those who could not be indentified a large cemetery was laid out in Flossenbürg. Remarkably, this expansion of the memorial led to the destruction of some of the remains of the concentration camp—the disinfection building was pulled down to make room for the cemetery. Moreover, the aesthetic design of this Grove of Honor (*Ehrenhain*) was that of a military cemetery. Thus a further blurring of the dimensions of the former concentration camp took place and once again an ahistorical interpretation of the camp dead was handed down. Minimizing the camp's remaining buildings maximized the decontextualized meaning attributed to the site. A "victims collective," formed out of the symbols of the military cemetery, reconciled and united a variety of vastly different perpectives: a topos of war victims. This way of dealing with murdered concentration camp prisoners was paradigmatic for the social consciouness of the Federal Republic of Germany up to the mid-1960s.

In Flossenbürg this consciousness took on a symbolic form that can still be seen today. With the addition of the cemetery, the Flossenbürg memorial was defined from this point on as both a memorial and burial-ground (Grab- und *Gedenkstätte*). Furthermore, as far as design and administration were concerned, it was treated as a cemetery. Transferring the remains of the death-march victims from the places were they were discovered also centered the memorial process in Flossenbürg and optically, it reduced remembrance to traditional forms of honoring the dead.

A qualitative turning-point in the development of the memorial came about with the planned demolition of the camp prison by the Flossenbürg local authority in 1964. For the first time there was a large protest against further destruction of historical buildings, mainly from French survivors of the camp and the Protestant Church, because it was here that Dietrich Bonhoefer must have spent the last night before his execution. After heated discussions, a rather unsatisfactory compromise was reached. It was decided to demolish three-quarters of the prison building. The rest was restored and in the rooms of this remaining section (*Restgefängnisses*) a small exhibition was set up dealing with the concentration camp. There were no further alterations to the Flossenbürg memorial until 1995. All the elements of the memorial that took shape up to 1995 can be seen today.

The memorial projects that had been realized had a decisive effect on the reception of Flossenbürg Concentration Camp. They determined, in their conceptual and aesthetic forms of expression, the way in which the former camp was perceived up to the 1990s. Although the remains of the camp were systematically dismantled and destroyed, the state administration made efforts to preserve the content and aesthetic appearance of the "cemetery of honor" (*Ehrenfriedhof*) form of remembrance. Since the beginning of the 1960s the site had been given the official title "Concentration Camp Memorial and Burial-Ground" (*KZ-Grab- und Gedenkstätte*) and had been administered as a land holding and not as an institution. It was a place where one remembered the dead but there was no attempt to bring the concentration camp dead to the attention of the public. Literally the "silence of the graveyard" prevailed in Flossenbürg. However, outside the memorial area, buildings that were fundamental to the former camp remain in existence: the central administrative building of the SS, the prisoners' kitchen, the camp laundry containing the prisoners' bath, the roll call area, the SS canteen, a few workshops, and the houses of the SS leadership.

New Perpectives since 1995. The year 1995 marked a turning point in the remembrance culture of a reunified Germany and brought about a profound and continuous change in both the perception of Flossenbürg Concentration Camp and the structural content of the concentration camp memorial. In 1995 public and media interest was no longer directed just at the better-known camps and memorials. Following the chronology of liberation, the lesser-known prisons, satellite camps, and death-march routes were also included. The memorials found themselves exposed to competition from an alternative remembrance policy. For Flossenbürg this meant that the image of a forgotten camp was conveyed via the media and in discussion in such a way that a basic reevaluation of that image was demanded of the state authorities responsible for memorials. In addition the views of the camp survivors were, for the first time, perceived as possessing a great deal of political weight in the discussion about Flossenbürg Concentration Camp.

On April 23, 1995, the fiftieth anniversary of the camp's liberation, several hundred former prisoners travelled to the Flossenbürg camp, the place where they had suffered so much. Alicia Nitecki, whose grandfather had been a prisoner there, suggested to Jack Terry that they attend. Jack Terry agreed, bringing with him his daughter Debbie—who was in an advanced stage of pregnancy—to see the scenes of his incarceration.

During the course of the increased public discussion, the state of Bavaria—the official body responsible for the memorial—officially recognized for the first time the pressing need to take action in the light of new conceptions of remembrance. In the spring of 1996, fifty-one years after the liberation of Flossenbürg Concentration Camp, an academic department was opened in the memorial grounds. Since then the Flossenbürg Concentration Camp memorial has developed with a dynamism that previously would not have been thought possible. In 1997 a central area of the former camp was made over as a gift to the state of Bavaria to be included as part of the memorial—the prisoners' kitchen, which had been used commerically, the prison laundry and the roll call area between the two buildings. Similarly, the local authority in Flossenbürg presented the camp commandant's building to the memorial, thus including in the expansion a core area of the former camp. Not only parts of the former "protective custody" (*Schutzhaft*) prison but also an essential operations building of the SS were therefore added to the memorial.

In the next few years a comprehensive new conception of the Flossenbürg Concentration Camp memorial will take shape and the site has been classified by the German government as an area of national and international importance. One of the biggest challenges for the new conception will be how to deal with the traces left behind from the postwar use of the camp, in other words, to uncover and to some extent clear away the various levels of interpretation and meaning that have been deposited there.

However, these layers of meaning will also be used to some extent to construct a contemporary document commenting on earlier attempts in the German Federal Republic to construct memorials and present views of history. The new conception will not only deal with the aesthetic form of the camp area. Its prime concern will be to create an academic basis for research into the history of Flossenbürg Concentration Camp and the fate of over one hundred thousand prisoners. The first successful steps in this direction have already been taken. A data bank with the names of all prisoners and their biographies is being created and in addition, the memorial now has at its disposal a substantial archive on the history of the Flossenbürg camp and its postwar reception. An external exhibition makes the memorial site accessible using new didactic methods and new developments in museum presentation. Reflections on the future of the Flossenbürg memorial are just beginning to develop. The new conception gives particular importance to the few remaining survivors of the terror of the Flossenbürg camp. They also have ideas and wishes with respect to the future design and appearance of the memorial. Their judgement will carry special weight in all further projects.

Since 1995 Jack Terry has returned many times to Flossenbürg and contributes to the process of developing the new conception with his reflective, constructive, and critical commitment. He has become a source of integration for the former prisoners. This is all the more remarkable and important when one considers the fact that an international committee of former Flossenbürg prisoners has never been founded. The publication of Alicia Nitecki and Jack Terry's book in the United States is a further decisive contribution to the uncovering of the real significance of Flossenbürg.

Jörg Skriebeleit, M.A., Archivist
Grab- und Gedenkstätte Flossenbürg

Notes

1. James E. Young. *Formen des Erinnerns*. Vienna 1997, p. 203. (English title: *The Texture of Memory: Holocaust Memorial and Meaning*. New Haven, CT: Yale University Press, 1993).

2. James E. Young. The Texture of Memory: Holocaust, Memorial and Meaning. New Haven, CT: Yale University Press, 1993.

3. Harold Marcuse. *Legacies of Dachau: The Use and Abuse of a Concentration Camp, 1933–2001.* Cambridge: Cambridge University Press, 2001.

4. Aleida Assmann. *Erinnerungsräume.* Munich, 1999, p. 328.

5. James E. Young. *Formen des Erinnerns.* Vienna, 1997, p. 113.

6. Ludwig Göhring. *Dachau, Flossenbürg Neuengamme, eine antifaschistische Biographie.* GNN, Schkeuditz, 1999, p. 222.

7. Wolfgang Sofsky. *The order of terror.*

8. *The Sniper,* April 26, 1945. Since 1995, a discussion has taken place between veterans associations of the 90th and 97 Infantry Divisions about who liberated Flossenbürg Concentration Camp similar to that between the 45th and 42nd Infantry Divisions concerning the liberation of Dachau Concentration Camp; cf. Robert W. Hacker: Flossenbürg Concentration Camp, Phoenix 2000, unpublished manuscript. Flossenbürg memorial archive, Lib.

9. NARA; RG 260; 13/147-2, p. 69F.

10. On May 1, 1945 a remembrance ceremony was held on the roll call ground "to celebrate the liberation of the inmates and the Russian national holiday." NARA, RG 260, 13/147-2, p. 70.

11. Frank Stern. *Im Anfang war Auschwitz.* Gerlingen, 1991, p. 62

12. It is unclear whether the expression had already been used by the concentration camp prisoners.